The Boer War

A Captivating Guide to Its Causes, Battles, and Legacy in South Africa

© Copyright 2024 - All rights reserved.

The content contained within this book may not be reproduced, duplicated, or transmitted without direct written permission from the author or the publisher.

Under no circumstances will any blame or legal responsibility be held against the publisher, or author, for any damages, reparation, or monetary loss due to the information contained within this book, either directly or indirectly.

Legal Notice:

This book is copyright protected. It is only for personal use. You cannot amend, distribute, sell, use, quote, or paraphrase any part, or the content within this book, without the consent of the author or publisher.

Disclaimer Notice:

Please note the information contained within this document is for educational and entertainment purposes only. All effort has been executed to present accurate, up-to-date, reliable, and complete information. No warranties of any kind are declared or implied. Readers acknowledge that the author is not engaging in the rendering of legal, financial, medical, or professional advice. The content within this book has been derived from various sources. Please consult a licensed professional before attempting any techniques outlined in this book.

By reading this document, the reader agrees that under no circumstances is the author responsible for any losses, direct or indirect, that are incurred as a result of the use of the information contained within this document, including, but not limited to, errors, omissions, or inaccuracies.

Free Bonus from Captivating History (Available for a Limited time)

Hi History Lovers!

Now you have a chance to join our exclusive history list so you can get your first history ebook for free as well as discounts and a potential to get more history books for free!

Simply visit the link below to join.

Or, Scan the QR code!

captivatinghistory.com/ebook

Also, make sure to follow us on Facebook, X, and YouTube by searching for Captivating History.

Table of Contents

INTRODUCTION 1
CHAPTER 1 – THE CREATION OF AN EMPIRE 4
CHAPTER 2 – SOUTH AFRICA AND THE BOERS 8
CHAPTER 3 – BUILDUP TO WAR 14
CHAPTER 4 – THE BATTLEFIELD AND THE OPPONENTS 27
CHAPTER 5 – THE FIRST PHASE: BOERS ON THE ATTACK 33
CHAPTER 6 – RELIEVING THE SIEGES: KIMBERLEY, LADYSMITH, AND MAFEKING 42
CHAPTER 7 – THE SECOND PHASE: THE EMPIRE STRIKES BACK 67
CHAPTER 8 – THE THIRD PHASE: GUERRILLA WARFARE 81
CHAPTER 9 – DEFEAT 87
CONCLUSION 90
CHRONOLOGY 93
TERMINOLOGY 95
DRAMATIS PERSONAE 97
HERE'S ANOTHER BOOK BY CAPTIVATING HISTORY THAT YOU MIGHT LIKE 100
FREE BONUS FROM CAPTIVATING HISTORY (AVAILABLE FOR A LIMITED TIME) 101

Introduction

As the end of the 19th century drew to a close, the British Empire presided over a vast collection of colonies and dominions. Underpinned by a powerful navy, the empire stretched across the globe, encompassing Canada, Africa, the Indian subcontinent, East Asia, Australia, and New Zealand.

South Africa was one area of strong British influence. However, the region was home to a complicated mix of British, Boers (a mix of primarily Dutch and German settlers), and many native tribes, all competing for different goals. After many local tribal clashes, the British attempted to subjugate the biggest tribal threat—the Zulus—in 1879. This was successful, but it came at a great cost. What's more, in 1881, the British Army was humiliatingly defeated by a small force of Boers and forced to strike a peace agreement.

This allowed the Boers to form their own independent republics: the Transvaal (also known as the South African Republic) and the Orange Free State. But Britain was still pressing hard to bring the disparate states in South Africa under its control into some form of South African union that was self-governing but under British stewardship. The Boers wanted nothing more than to be left alone.

The discovery of diamonds in South Africa in the 1860s and then gold in the 1870s triggered a flood of migrants in search of riches. They overwhelmed the Boer society and demanded their own voting rights. With these valuable assets, the Boer republics increasingly looked tempting to Britain. A bigger war between the British and the Boers was brewing. Provoked by unrealistic political demands, the Boers decided to act first, launching attacks against the unprepared British forces.

The British Empire stumbled, suffering heavily before regaining ground through sheer manpower and resources. However, there would be two and a half years of bitter fighting before the Boers finally succumbed.

Is this the last colonial war or the first modern war?

It was a curious mix of adversaries fighting during the period of the colonial high-water mark just before the First World War. The British and Boers had a common European heritage, and both had access to the same modern European weapons. However, their history, culture, and tactics were very different. Although the British had superior numbers, the Boers fought with skill, determination, and flexibility. They were highly mobile opponents.

This was a war that brutally impacted civilians—native Africans, women, and children—on a scale that took the world by surprise.

We will meet a diverse range of people in this story, including commanders from previous colonial tribal wars, such as Redvers Buller, and British officers who would later find fame during the First World War, such as Kitchener, Haig, and French. There were gritty, determined Boer commanders, such as Christian de Wet and Louis Botha, who fought desperately to preserve Boer statehood. We will also meet a young journalist named Winston Churchill and a British Army stretcher-bearer named Mahatma Gandhi.

We will witness the origins of many of the weapons, technologies, and concepts of the modern total war that was to come in the First and Second World Wars, including machine guns, trenches, barbed wire, artillery barrages, guerrilla warfare, refugees, and concentration camps.

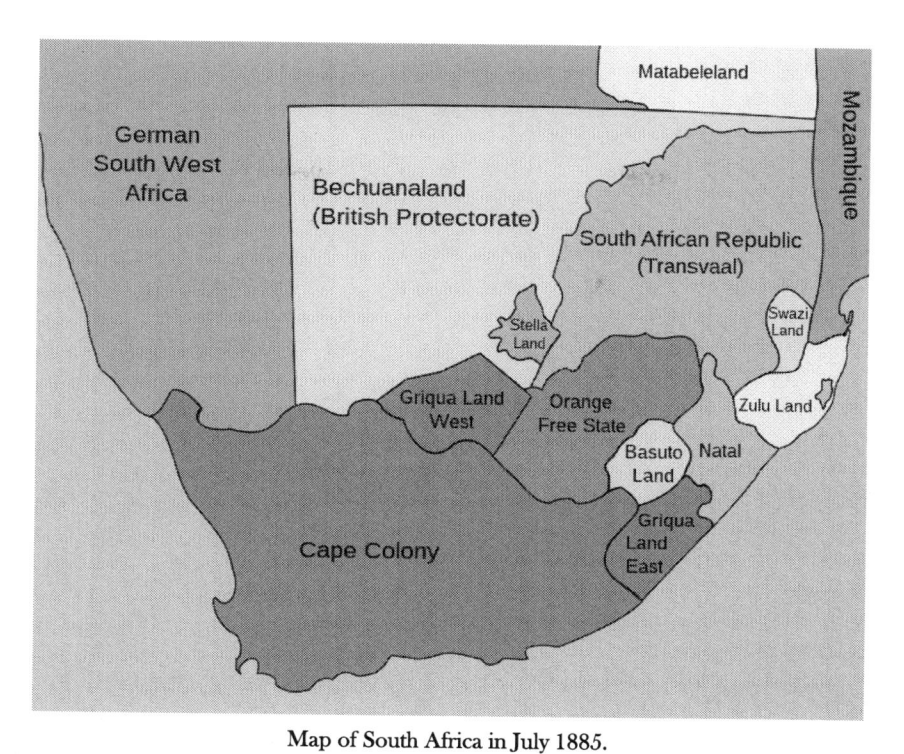

Map of South Africa in July 1885.
This file is licensed under the Creative Commons Attribution-Share Alike 3.0 Unported license.
https://en.wikipedia.org/wiki/File:SouthAfrica1885.svg

Chapter 1 – The Creation of an Empire

The Sun Never Sets...
What became known as the "British Empire" started from very humble beginnings about three centuries before it reached what might be considered its peak in the early part of the 20th century. Britain, through its development and maintenance of a powerful maritime presence and, later, a formal navy, developed trading routes, trading posts, settlements, and small-scale colonies from the 16th century onward. In 1600, the East India Trading Company was established in the Indian subcontinent. There were intense trading rivalries and often wars, but the Dutch East India Company was powerful and profitable during the 17th century.

As Britain pushed westward to the Americas, it was often in competition with other imperial rivals, especially France and Spain. It was apparent that there were great opportunities to amass resources, riches, and power through the exploitation of the world beyond Europe, even if this meant cruelly mishandling the natives who already lived there. In this respect, European access to weapons and technologies gave would-be colonizers a significant head start as they sought to carve out swathes of territory in the names of the various kings and queens of Europe.

British conquests accelerated in the 17th century, with major gains being made in North America and the West Indies. France was a major rival in North America until the Treaty of Paris in 1763 brought an end to the Seven Years' War between Britain and France, effectively giving Britain control over North America, including former French possessions.

However, only three decades later, Britain lost its control of North America. A bitter and costly war on the east coast saw American colonists reject British rule and declare independence. This loss was painful to the British Crown and gave it a strong lesson in the risks of pushing colonial subjects too hard.

But there were some compensations. Britain gained Canada and Australia. It also made substantial gains at the expense of France as a result of the Napoleonic Wars.

Challenges of Running an Empire

From a small section of the Home Office in central London, the Colonial Office was formed in 1801. During the course of the 19th century, it took on more and more administrative power and responsibility for running the empire. This was a complex and costly business, although it became slightly easier in the latter half of the 19th century as the speed of steam-powered shipping increased and the invention of the telegraph allowed messages to be transmitted and read almost instantly.

Imperial subjects across the globe were not always content with being ruled by London. The risk of rebellion was very real, and it was not easy to judge where, when, and why outbreaks of violent protest might take place.

At its peak, the British East India Company had control over 250,000 armed soldiers. The British Army was still relatively small, focused on preventing small tribal uprisings and colonial frontier skirmishes. It mustered a modest force of approximately 350,000 soldiers, while the European "continental armies" (France, Germany, and Russia) could, in theory, put millions into the field. With such a relatively small force and a quarter of the globe to cover, Britain was dependent on the Royal Navy and its maritime trading reach to be able to move reinforcements and resources quickly to deal with any troublesome regions. However, the British did not always get it right. The Zulu War in 1879 and the Second Boer War, which took place twenty years later, were examples of the British troops on the ground being inadequate for the job and having to wait weeks before reinforcements could come to the rescue.

The late 19th century saw a rapid expansion of imperial interests in Africa on the part of the British, French, German, Portuguese, and others. This was known as the "Scramble for Africa," in which large chunks of Africa were sliced up and divided amongst the governments of Europe. At the end of this period, Britain boasted major gains across the continent, including Egypt, Sudan, Nigeria, Ghana, Kenya, Uganda, South Africa, Zambia, and Malawi. The aspiration amongst many British imperialists at that time (particularly Cecil Rhodes) was for a British-controlled railway line to link all the British possessions from the "Cape to Cairo."

The British Empire was continually troubled by armed conflict and resistance, literally from A to Z—from American colonists to the Zulu—as it sought to maintain power and influence. Some were full-blown independence movements, while others were minor skirmishes over specific local issues of governance, particular rules, or cultural principles. Here are but a few examples:

1775-1782 - American War of Independence

1786 - Chargola Uprising (in India against the East India Company)

1798 - Irish Rebellion

1808-1810 - Rum Rebellion (Australia)

1817-1818 - Paika Rebellion (in India against the East India Company)

1839-1842 - First Anglo-Afghan War

1857 - Indian Mutiny

1867 - Fenian Rising (Ireland)

1878-1880 - Second Anglo-Afghan War

1879 - Anglo-Zulu War

1881 - First Boer War

1881-1899 - Mahdist War (Sudan)

1899-1902 - Second Boer War

1919 - Third Anglo-Afghan War

1919-1921 - Irish War of Independence

1936-1936 - Arab revolt in Palestine

1944-1948 - Zionist resistance in Palestine

1952-1960 - Mau Mau rebellion (Kenya)

Height of Power

It is difficult to judge exactly when the British Empire was at the height of its power, but the end of the 19th and the beginning of the 20th century is a reasonable assessment. In the contemporary British school atlases at the time, almost a third of the globe was colored red, symbolizing the British Empire's dominance. The global sprawl of the empire ensured that at any time of the day, somewhere in the world, the sun was shining on the empire, whether it was Canada, the West Indies, Africa, the Indian subcontinent, Southeast Asia, Australia, New Zealand, or the Pacific Ocean. Around four hundred million people were, whether they liked it or not, part of the British Empire.

The Situation in 1899

In Britain in 1899, a hypothetical government civil servant in the Foreign or Colonial Office would have been aware of several challenges facing the empire. Not everyone was comfortable with the empire's policies, particularly the poor treatment of African tribes. The situation in Ireland was also becoming increasingly divisive. Irish nationalists were seeking to break away from the empire, and Protestant Unionists were determined to remain a part of the United Kingdom, even if it came to armed insurrection. New empires, such as the United States and Japan, were providing additional competition. The political and security situation in South Africa was once again threatening to move toward violence (after the Zulu War in 1879 and the First Boer War in 1881). Although domestic popular opinion was still broadly supportive of the empire, a serious confrontation in South Africa, which had been brewing for some time, was about to provide a serious test to both the government and the British people.

Chapter 2 – South Africa and the Boers

Geography and Climate
South Africa is a semi-arid region with a temperate climate characterized by sweeping savannahs and stark mountain ranges. The Highveld is a high inland plateau that is generally higher than five thousand feet. A dominant feature there is the Drakensberg mountain range. Ridges, mountains, and deep valleys are common in the Highveld. We will encounter two major rivers during this account of the Boer War. The Orange River is the longest in South Africa, flowing east to west from Lesotho to the Atlantic Ocean, a distance of some 1,300 miles. The Tugela River is the largest river but is shorter, being around 312 miles in length, and flows through Natal from west to east into the Indian Ocean. In the late 19th century, it was also a geopolitical boundary, forming a border between British Natal and the Zulu Kingdom.

Most of South Africa is at a fairly high altitude. It is generally cooler in the west and warmer in the east. The summers (from December to February) are warm to hot and the winters (from June to August) are cool to cold. It is rare to have extremes, but temperatures at the higher altitudes can drop from the mid-20s during the day down to below freezing at night.

There are a wide variety of minerals in South Africa. Two discoveries in the 19th century had a bearing on political, social, and economic aspects of the region before, during, and after the Anglo-Boer War.

Diamonds were discovered in and around Kimberley in the 1860s. Very extensive and pure gold deposits were found in the Witwatersrand cliffs range north of Johannesburg in the 1880s. The gold mines became a prominent cause of the war.

Dutch Origins

The Dutch first recognized the potential for the southern tip of Africa when a shipwrecked Dutch crew saw the extensive natural resources available. This was reported back to the Netherlands, and a Dutch East India Trading Company expedition confirmed that the area could be very useful—essential even—to base a colony there in order to provide a replenishment station (meat, vegetables, fruit) for ships traveling between the Netherlands and the Dutch East Indies. Dutch settlers consequently established themselves in the Cape of Good Hope around 1652. Many wanted to escape the wars and persecution afflicting western Europe at the time. The settlement, known as Cape Town, became a place for former employees of the Dutch East India Company to retire. They could rent land and grow crops. It stayed under the control of the Dutch East India Company for well over a hundred years, but increasing conflicts with the British, who also saw the value of a colony at the midway mark to India, made its tenure precarious.

Taken by the British

In August 1795, a British fleet landed on the Cape of Good Hope and captured the town. Cape Town was returned to the Dutch after a peace treaty in 1802, but it was lost again to the British in 1806 during the Napoleonic Wars. Another British invasion fleet fought and conquered the town. At this time and for the first half of the 19th century, the South African colony was seen as having little economic value itself but remained a valuable staging point.

By the time the Cape Colony was taken by the British, there were twenty-six thousand settlers in the town, predominantly of Dutch origin. But there were many others as well, including Germans and French Huguenots. After the British took control, British settlers began to arrive in the colony. The name "Boer" comes from the Dutch word for farmer, and this mix of Dutch, German, and French settlers were strongly religious communities, living strictly according to the tenets of the Bible and preferring to live an independent lifestyle, working their own isolated farms and their own territories. They preferred the far-flung frontiers, where they were dependent on agriculture and hunting, to urban life. They believed they had a God-given right to the land and also the right to exploit the African natives who lived there.

As Cape Town expanded and political control became more deep-seated, the Boers increasingly resented British control and began to leave, traveling in columns of horse-drawn wagons and pushing out into the unchartered land to the east—rather like the American pioneers driving west in the United States in the 19th century. This Boer quest to find their own plots of land free from monarchic or political interference became known as "trekking." This took them beyond the reach of British governance and into areas already settled by numerous local African tribes. This triggered regular border disputes, clashes, and a series of conflicts called the Frontier Wars over the next hundred years, most notably with the Xhosa people. The ninth and last Frontier War ended in 1878.

During many of these conflicts, the British and Boers—as white Europeans—cooperated and fought together against local African tribes. Thus, the boundaries of the Cape Colony gradually and semi-officially expanded to the north, northeast, and east, despite the efforts of the Cape government to establish agreed borders and minimize the risks of armed conflict. As the Boers forged eastward, they began to establish their own colonies and "republics." Some lasted little more than months, while others endured for decades. Few survived to see the start of the 20th century.

The Great Trek

British rule over the Boers was unpopular. In the 1830s, the relations between the British and the Boers deteriorated greatly. The British abolition of slavery in the colony on December 1st, 1834, became a major cause of discontent for the Boers, who were dependent economically upon the use of slaves. Other administrative and religious issues also drove the Boers away from British rule. From 1835 to 1846, around fourteen thousand Boer men, women, and children—*Voortrekkers* (pioneers)—set out from the eastern edge of the Cape Colony and crossed the Orange River, traveling north in covered wagons. They were determined to establish their own homeland away from British influence. This caused alarm, friction, and clashes with the indigenous peoples who already lived in the areas now being occupied by the Boers.

A concept propagated at the time was the "Vacant Land Theory," which held that the land the Boers were moving into was empty, thus legitimizing the Boers' conquest of the land. This was controversial, and the current South African government points to the lack of archaeological and historical evidence to support this claim. The Vacant Land Theory is now dismissed as a myth.

The Boers' use of muzzle-loading guns was crucial to the Great Trek, and several actions went in favor of the small, outnumbered Boer groups because of this modern form of firepower. In October 1836, the Potgieter Boer expedition confronted the Ndebele tribe; there were forty trekkers against up to six thousand Ndebele warriors. In mid-December 1838, the Boers were attacked by the forces under Zulu Chief Dingane at the Battle of Blood River. In a fight that quickly passed into Boer folklore, less than five hundred Voortrekkers under Andries Pretorius tightly circled their wagons and used disciplined gunfire to fight off over ten thousand Zulu warriors. As many as three thousand Zulus were reported to be killed in the encounter. Only three Boer fighters were lightly wounded.

The Boer Republics Are Established

With the successful defense against the Zulus, the Boers established their own Republic of Natalia. However, it would not last long. In 1843, the British caught up with the Boers and annexed the republic. Other Boer republics established during this mass migration include the Transvaal (otherwise known as the South African Republic), which was founded in 1852, and the Orange Free State in 1854. These two republics were formally recognized by the British—for a while at least.

The British in the Cape Colony and Natal existed in a state of uneasy coexistence with the Boer Republics of Transvaal and the Orange Free State. The Boers did not trust the British and were always on the alert for provocations.

The First Anglo-Boer War

In the 1870s, the British policy regarding South Africa was to bring all the various states, colonies, and republics—British, Boers, and Africans—into one British-controlled self-governing confederation of South Africa. This policy had been successful in Canada. Lord Carnarvon became the Conservative Party's secretary of state for the colonies. In 1876, Carnarvon's advice to the Conservative prime minister, Benjamin Disraeli, was that this could and should be quickly achieved, if necessary, by acting with force.

In 1877, Britain annexed the Transvaal. There was no significant resistance to this at the time. There were several reasons for that. The Boer government was in a poor financial situation since they were fighting a war with the Pei African tribe. There were also serious disputes and land feuds with the Zulus in the borderlands between the Transvaal and the Zulu Kingdom. On April 12th, 1877, the Transvaal was annexed and became a British colony.

Although there was limited resistance to this move at the time, the Boers were not happy and presented a petition to London expressing their unhappiness.

The British engineered a war with King Cetwayo and the powerful Zulu Kingdom east of Natal. The war lasted from January to July 1879. The British Army was arrogant and over-confident. It also lacked vital knowledge of the terrain and the enemy. Due to a combination of poor planning and poor intelligence, a well-armed column of troops under Lord Chelmsford was dealt a costly and embarrassing defeat at Isandlwana by Zulu forces that were armed predominantly with spears. Other reverses followed, and the British withdrew in confusion. It was only months later, after a massive new injection of troops, artillery, and machine guns, that the British forces were able to gain victory over the Zulus and annex the kingdom.

In December 1880, following a tax dispute with the British, the Transvaal Boers staged an uprising, and an armed conflict broke out. To their surprise, the British got the worst of it, with many of their Transvaal garrisons suddenly under siege. The Boers were well armed with modern breech-loading rifles (unlike the spear-armed Zulus the British had just defeated). Their tactics were well thought out; they relied on accurate shooting from a long distance and did not charge in a solid mass straight into British firepower. The Boers were also highly mobile, operating when possible from horseback. The British were still transitioning from bright red, highly visible tunics to khaki material, the latter of which would define the British Army color scheme until well after the Second World War. Not all soldiers had been issued the new uniforms.

Compared to the battles of the Zulu War and what was to come twenty years later in the Second Boer War, the battles with the Boers were not large. Most battles were Boer ambushes of British supply columns and lines of communications. The Boers showed great pragmatism, choosing not to engage in hand-to-hand combat or to storm well-defended positions unless necessary. Boer snipers took a heavy toll on the prominent British officers as they waved swords and pistols on the front line, urging the British soldiers forward.

The rebuffs dealt to the British were enough to push the government toward negotiations. On February 14th, 1880, the fighting stopped, and peace talks were set to begin. However, by either miscalculation or misunderstanding, Major General Sir George Colley, the governor of Natal and the commander of the British troops, launched another attack on the Boers on February 27th. He might have been attempting to improve the British bargaining position.

The resultant Battle of Majuba Hill was a resounding defeat for the British. Although the British took the hill, a sharp Boer counterattack caused the British to flee in disarray. General Colley was spared the embarrassment of an inquiry and possible dismissal; he was shot dead by a Boer sniper while trying to rally his troops. He was one of the 92 British killed (along with 134 injured and 59 prisoners).

An armistice was signed on March 6th, 1880, and the Transvaal was given self-governance. In 1884, the London Convention gave the Transvaal full independence.

Majuba Hill was a shameful moment in British military history. "Remember Majuba" was a rallying cry used by the British during the Second Boer War. Twenty years later, many of the lessons learned by the British appeared to have been forgotten. For the Boers, it was an inspirational example of what they could achieve in an armed confrontation with the British.

The First Boer War was prominent in the minds of the Boer political and military leaders, many of whom had served during the buildup to the 1899 conflict.

Chapter 3 – Buildup to War

South Africa had generally been seen as a vital transport stepping stone to India and beyond. It was a strategically valuable refueling and trading post, but it had little other value. It was the only viable route from Europe to the Indian subcontinent and beyond, certainly in the days before the Suez Canal had been built. For centuries, it had not been seen as a major economic prize in its own right. This began to change in the latter part of the 19th century and was to have a significant impact on political dynamics in the region.

In the late 1860s, diamonds were discovered on the banks of the Orange River. Mining exploration expanded rapidly, and by the 1880s, a major mining town called Kimberley had sprung up and was producing over 90 percent of the world's diamonds, bringing much wealth to the Cape Colony's economy. British political sleight of hand had initially ruled that the area was part of Griqualand, a small, largely powerless mixed-race sub-group, which was subsequently annexed into the British Cape Colony in 1877.

The De Beers mining company was formed at Kimberley by Cecil John Rhodes, a larger-than-life character who shared many imperial visions of British expansion and the desire to exploit cheap native African labor forces.

Gold in Witwatersrand and Uitlanders

In the middle of the 1880s, gold was discovered in a farming area in the Witwatersrand ("White Water Ridge") region in the Boer Transvaal Republic. It was not the purest kind, but the quality was reliable and in huge quantities. Cecil Rhodes and other wealthy investors were quick to establish mining companies.

However, this brought bad news for the Boers. A "gold rush" of opportunists, prospectors, fortune seekers, businessmen, and industrialists from Europe and all over the world poured into the Transvaal, threatening to overwhelm the smaller Boer communities. Many British came from the Cape Colony and the United Kingdom.

The mines were deep, and the work of digging out the gold was difficult, unpleasant, and very dangerous. It proved difficult to get black African laborers to work in the mines. At one point, fifty thousand Chinese made up a large part of the labor force. Shanty towns sprang up, bringing a whole range of human behaviors that shocked the deeply religious Boers. People in these crude and rowdy shanty communities gambled, drank alcohol, and engaged in prostitution, crime, and violence.

The city of Johannesburg was founded in 1886 and expanded rapidly due to the surge of people seeking work. Within ten years, Johannesburg had a population of 100,000. These immigrants into the Transvaal became known as "Uitlanders" (foreigners or outsiders). There were so many of them that the Boers were fearful they would become the majority. Their arrival and demands would become a major cause of the turbulence that led to the Second Boer War.

Paul Kruger

The Boer president of the Transvaal at the time was Stephanus Johannes Paulus Kruger, better known as Paul Kruger. The Kruger family tree boasted French, German, and Dutch blood, and the Krugers had been in South Africa since 1713.

Paul Kruger was greatly respected by the Boer people. He was affectionately nicknamed "Oom Paul" (Uncle Paul). He was born in 1825. At the age of eleven, he and his family became part of the original Voortrekkers and took part in the Great Trek in 1836. He took part in some of the battles against African tribes. As a young boy, he supported the adult fighters by helping to cast bullets. He grew up to be a horseman, a farmer, and a marksman.

The deeply and strictly religious Kruger was almost the embodiment of the history of his people, and he was devoted to protecting them. He became the president of the South African Republic four times. He was a legend, although at this stage, in his sixties, his health was failing somewhat. In the late 1870s, he was highly active in trying to get the British to reverse their annexation of the Transvaal. The arrival of the Uitlanders and the deterioration of the Boers' relationship with Britain were his greatest problems by the mid-1880s.

Rivalries and Demand for Rights

One of Kruger's difficulties was the Uitlanders' demand for civil and political rights in the Transvaal. They especially pushed for their right to vote. The discovery of diamonds and gold in the Transvaal threatened to destabilize the region. It was now suddenly richer and, therefore, potentially more powerful than the British-controlled Cape Colony. In 1979, the historian Thomas Packenham summarized the dilemma that was slowly emerging:

"Quite suddenly the Cape and the Transvaal seemed to be exchanging roles, as political leadership of the sub-continent passed to the Transvaal. There was now a double anomaly about the two states. The Cape was a British colony, though the majority of the white inhabitants were Afrikaners; the Transvaal was still a Boer republic, though it appeared the majority of its inhabitants were, by the mid-1890s, British, for the gold-rush had sucked in so many British immigrants. Who, then, was to control the Transvaal, richest state in Africa?"[1]

Cecil Rhodes had his own ideas about that.

Cecil Rhodes and the Jameson Raid

Cecil John Rhodes was born in England in 1853 to an affluent family. He was well educated and well read, but he was plagued with ill health throughout his relatively short life (he died in 1902 at the age of forty-eight). When he was seventeen, he was sent to South Africa to visit his older brother Herbert in the hope that the climate would be good for him and that he might be able to develop a career there under his brother's guidance. He showed considerable aptitude for business and brought £3,000 of the family's savings with him with the intention that he should make some investments.

After working on his brother's farm, he moved to the Kimberley region in 1871 to explore the potential of the diamond mines that were springing up. He also became attracted to the possibilities of the lands farther north: Bechuanaland and the region that would become

---

[1] Pakenham, T., *The Boer War*, (Abacus: London 2022), p. 21.

Zimbabwe. He returned briefly to England to study at Oxford and came back to South Africa with strong ideas about the superiority of the Anglo-Saxon race, the English, and the British Empire. He became an ardent imperialist and felt that the British Empire should dominate the world.

"I contend that we are the first race in the world, and that the more of the world we inhabit the better it is for the human race. Just fancy those parts that are at present inhabited by the most despicable specimen of human being, what an alteration there would be in them if they were brought under Anglo-Saxon influence ... if there be a God, I think that what he would like me to do is paint as much of the map of Africa British Red as possible."[2]

Rhodes entered the diamond trade in 1871 and quickly made an impact. He started buying up other mines—he had secured financial support from the Rothschild company—and was able to accelerate the buy-out process in the mid-1870s when the diamond industry was in something of a slump. Rhodes stayed the course; by 1890, he had established almost a complete monopoly.

He did not stop there. He next diversified his career. In 1881, at the age of twenty-seven, Rhodes entered the Cape Colony political system, becoming prime minister in 1890. His policies were anti-black African. He increased the wealth criteria for the right to vote, which meant most Africans were excluded from the political process.

With his vision of expanding the territories of the British Empire, he began to look north and northeast. He was already fixing in his mind the idea of a new swathe of imperial expansion that would link the Cape of Good Hope to Cairo, including by railway and telegraph. This was the idea of a "red line," with British interests no longer dependent upon negotiating with other nations for passage, communications, or transportation at any point from the Mediterranean down to the South Atlantic.

Rhodes's aggressive focus, political influence, and financial assets made him appear unstoppable. Bechuanaland became a British protectorate, and it was largely policed by mounted police units of Rhodes's British South Africa Company (BSAC). From the early 1890s,

---

[2] "Cecil John Rhodes," *South African History Online*, website accessed 27 Nov. 2023, https://www.sahistory.org.za/people/cecil-john-rhodes.

the area gradually became known as "Rhodesia."

But what of the two Boer republics? Rhodes's own vision of the empire and his personal business interests would have been greatly served if the Transvaal and the Orange Free State were returned to British control. He took a strong interest in the plight of the Uitlanders. The Boers were not treating them well, denying many of them the right to vote. The Boers feared the dominating numbers of enfranchised adult male Uitlanders would vote to overturn Boer culture. The issue was generating tension, unhappiness, and protest. Rhodes was determined to exploit this. In 1895, he conceived of a plan to seize control of the Transvaal.

Rhodes would use his own BSAC mounted infantry units and make a quick armed sally from just across the border with the Transvaal. The troopers—little more than six hundred strong—would support a concurrent armed uprising by Uitlanders inside Johannesburg. This two-pronged attack would knock out the Boer government and replace it with something more suitable to both Rhodes and the British government.

One of the real controversies of the plan was the extent to which the British government in London knew about the plot. Rhodes seemed to believe he had the tacit backing of the secretary of state for the colonies, Joseph Chamberlain. Chamberlain would later deny all knowledge of the affair; it would, of course, have been extremely damaging to his reputation and the government if Britain had been engaged in plotting a coup.

In late December 1895, the Rhodesian troopers of Rhodes's private army were gathered at Pitsani, waiting for the order to go. An uprising would be started in Johannesburg by Uitlander reformers, and this would be the signal for the Rhodesian force to quickly ride in and reestablish law and order. If they could take control of a Boer armory, they could then distribute the weapons to the Uitlanders and develop the uprising further.

The force was led by Dr. Leander Jameson and supported by several ex-British Army officers who shared Rhodes's grandiose visions and were also still smarting from the defeat dished out at Majuba. They had a small selection of Maxim machine guns and light artillery pieces. The officers and the troopers were experienced, having fought several campaigns against Africans in Matabeleland (just north of the Transvaal).

But not so much Jameson. He was a qualified doctor and became an administrator in one of Rhodes's business companies.

On the eve of the attack, the news came from Johannesburg that the Uitlander uprising was becoming less likely. The reformist Uitlanders were starting to argue amongst themselves and were less willing to commit to violence. The message was that the coup was off.

Jameson, kicking his heels in the dusty middle of nowhere, grew increasingly impatient. He made the crucial and fatal decision to proceed anyway, which he communicated to Rhodes by telegram on December 28th, 1895. On December 29th, the force set out into the Transvaal. They cut down the telegraph wires to avoid Johannesburg being alerted.

Apparently, as an apocryphal story relates, they missed cutting an important cable—the one that led to Pretoria—because some of the troopers were drunk. They cut down some farm fencing instead. It is probable that this error caused the Boers to be warned of the danger.

Either way, it was not long before the Boers were alerted, and armed mounted contingents of Boers came forward to confront the British. The forlorn force headed off to its uncertain fate. For a mission that depended on speed and surprise, the venture was more or less over before it had started.

There was no grand, glorious battle. A series of small-scale but bitter skirmishes gradually took its toll on the Rhodesian police troopers over the course of four days. More Boer fighters kept arriving to slow the advance. There was a larger confrontation at Krugersdorp, which lasted several hours, where the Boers had time to dig trenches and defensive positions.

Jameson swung south and tried to bypass the Boers' line of defense. Eventually, Jameson and his force found themselves surrounded at Doornkop. This was to be the last stand. With sixty-five dead and wounded (more than 10 percent of his force), ammunition low, and most of the officers killed or wounded, the group raised the white apron of an African servant girl as a flag of surrender. Jameson was captured and led away in tears.

There were some immediate combat lessons for all to see. The Boers, who were adept at marksmanship, creating trenches, and concealment had barely been visible to the beleaguered Jameson group and had only suffered one death.

Aftermath of the Jameson Raid

Many historians and analysts have subsequently come to see the Jameson Raid as the starting point of the Boer War. Chamberlain and Rhodes scrambled to distance themselves from the abortive coup. The British public opinion was mixed; some were embarrassed and angry, while others saw Jameson as a patriotic hero. Jameson was lucky to escape execution at the hands of the Boers, but President Kruger was keen to avoid inflaming an already tense and volatile situation. The last thing he wanted at this point was a British martyr.

Jameson, along with the other conspirators, was briefly imprisoned in Pretoria, but they were later sent back to the British in England for trial there. He received fifteen months in Holloway prison. The Transvaal-based co-conspirators (which included Cecil Rhodes's own brother, Frank, a colonel in the British Army) were also rounded up and received harsh sentences.

Kaiser Wilhelm II sent a telegram to President Kruger on January 3rd to offer his congratulations on the defeat of the raid. This further exacerbated the situation; Britain was now highly sensitive to the idea of German support for the Boer republics.[3] Ultimately, Leander Jameson did not fare too badly. He was very popular in London society after his release and eventually returned to South Africa. He became prime minister of the Cape Colony from 1904 to 1908.

Secretary of State Chamberlain narrowly escaped losing his job. It transpired that telegrams between himself and Rhodes implicated him much more deeply than had been suspected. In 1896, Rhodes was compelled to resign as the Cape Colony's prime minister and as director of the British South Africa Company. We will meet Cecil Rhodes again later in the Boer War, albeit under a very different set of circumstance.

The Boers had suffered a rude awakening. It served to unite them in adversity against a powerful enemy. However, it also showed them how poor the Boer military system was. It was one thing to fight small-scale skirmishes against spear-and-shield-equipped tribesmen and quite another to contest a battlefield with one of the most modern and powerful armies in the world. In a time of conflict, the Boers were

---

[3] "Kruger telegram," *Britannica*, website accessed 28 Nov. 2023, https://www.britannica.com/event/Kruger-telegram.

required to turn up with a horse, rations, a rifle, and ammunition. Boer citizens were more or less "invited" to take part and could discuss plans amongst themselves and come and go as they wished. It was a very democratic—and, therefore, somewhat hit-and-miss—approach to war. The Jameson force was a mere six hundred strong and relatively easy to deal with. But many of the Boers who had arrived to chase off the attack had no rifles, no ammunition, or very old equipment.

"There was only enough ammunition to make war for a fortnight. The country, concluded Kruger, was 'practically defenceless' at the time of the raid; 'the burghers had neglected their sacred duty to arm themselves.'"[4]

This became a key priority for Kruger. The Boers sought weapons from Europe – particularly Germany – and spent over a million pounds on military hardware. This included state-of-the-art Mauser bolt-action magazine-loading rifles and several million rounds. They acquired a range of light and heavy modern artillery pieces: Maxim "pom-pom" one-pounder machine guns that fired exploding bullets, 75mm Creusot artillery pieces that outranged their British equivalents, and 155mm "Long Tom" guns. For all the Boers' reputation as light mounted infantry, they quickly developed a powerful artillery corps as well. The British would come to fear and respect the Boer artillery in the years ahead.

The Boers also reviewed and revised the way they mobilized their troops. Eventually, they were confident they could mobilize up to twenty-five thousand men within two weeks and possibly as many as forty thousand.

Over the next three years, recrimination and suspicion fueled mutual hostility. Accidents and deliberate provocations made things worse. The Boer police force, the South African Republic Police, developed a reputation for mistreating black African communities and Uitlanders. At Christmas 1898, Tom Edgar, an Uitlander, was shot dead by a policeman. The exact circumstances were murky, but the police claimed that Edgar had been drunk and violent. The incident caused outrage amongst the Uitlanders, many of whom saw it as a deliberate attack against them. They increasingly began to appeal to the British

---

[4] Pakenham, T., *The Boer War*, (Abacus: London 2022), p. 41.

government for assistance. British imperialists in the Cape Colony and London saw the opportunity to turn the issue of rights for Uitlanders into something that could be exploited for the annexation of the two republics.

Milner's Plans

A new British high commissioner for Southern Africa arrived in Cape Town in 1897. Alfred Milner was a convinced imperialist. He had been a senior financial administrator in Egypt and, in 1892, had written what was seen as a definitive work, *England and Egypt*, which documented the success of the British imperial rule in Egypt. He had essentially been sent to South Africa to clear up the political debris after the bungled Jameson affair and to preside over the annexation of the Boer republics, which he thought was essential, inevitable, and time sensitive.

Milner took the task seriously. He spent time traveling in South Africa to learn about the cultures and languages. He planned to have discussions with Kruger about the rights of the Uitlanders.

With Milner's arrival, it was tempting for people to see that war was inevitable. Indeed, there are many parallels with the way in which a previous British high commissioner, Sir Henry Bartle Frere, less than twenty years earlier, had deliberately engineered a confrontation with the Zulus in order to go to war and dismantle their empire. This was certainly what many Boers feared. However, the British public and government opinions were mixed. There was certainly enthusiasm for expanding the empire, and the riches offered in the gold and diamond mines made a powerful case in their own right (certainly for Rhodes and his business colleagues). But there were many other issues distracting the government at home and abroad. The British Army was small and unprepared for any significant conflict. The appetite for war was not great.

The Bloemfontein Conference, June 1899

In late May 1899, a conference at Bloemfontein was convened at the initiation of President Steyn of the Orange Free State in order to resolve the differences between the Boers and the British. There were still significant tensions in the Transvaal, and at the heart of it were the rights of the Uitlander, the large and vocal non-Boer minority. In the buildup to the conference, Milner sent a letter on May 4th to the Colonial Office in London:

"The case for intervention is overwhelming. The only attempted answer is that things will right themselves if left alone. But, in fact, the policy of leaving things alone has been tried for years, and it has led to their going from bad to worse. It is not true that this is owing to the raid. They were going from bad to worse before the raid. We were on the verge of war before the raid, and the Transvaal was on the verge of revolution. The effect of the raid has been to give the policy of leaving things alone a new lease of life, and with the old consequences. The spectacle of thousands of British subjects kept permanently in the position of helots, constantly chafing under undoubted grievances, and calling vainly to her Majesty's Government for redress, does steadily undermine the influence and reputation of Great Britain within the Queen's dominions."[5]

The meeting took place at the Bloemfontein railway station from May 31st to June 5th. It was, understandably, a tense affair. Both Milner and Kruger realized that war was a very real possibility and that this was the last chance to preserve peace. Neither Kruger nor Milner were disposed to making many concessions. Because of the Jameson Raid, the Transvaal voters had brought Kruger back to the presidency with a large majority. His position was safe; his people had confidence in him and his ability to negotiate with the British. Even so, although Kruger was starting to conclude that war was inevitable, many senior Boers, including Jan Smuts, the state attorney, could not imagine the British would be so stupid as to provoke a war for the Uitlander cause.[6]

Three Unacceptable Demands

Milner's opening demands were three-fold and deliberately designed to be hard for the Boers to stomach. He required that the Boers pass a law allowing the Uitlanders to have the right to vote, that the English language be used in the Transvaal parliament (the Volksraad), and that any laws passed by the Volksraad should be approved by the British Parliament. Kruger made a show of concessions. He indicated he might be prepared to reduce the number of years an Uitlander had to live in the Transvaal before gaining the right to vote. Kruger wanted the Uitlanders to have lived in the Transvaal for seven years and to renounce

---

[5] Doyle, C., 'The Great Boer War,' Sep. 1902, https://www.gutenberg.org/files/3069/3069-h/3069-h.htm

[6] Pakenham, T., *The Boer War*, (Abacus: London 2022), p. 63.

British citizenship. Milner wanted it to be five years.[7]

There was no personal connection between the two men; both were from very different cultures and had very different life experiences. Kruger was deeply obstinate, and Milner was highly impatient. The discussion bounced back and forth with little genuine interest in engagement on either side. Minor concessions were dressed up as major proposals. It slowly became clear that the discussion was going nowhere.

"The curtain had already fallen at Bloemfontein. Kruger, his eyes watering, had stood there for the last time, repeating, 'It is our country you want.' Milner had closed the proceedings with the chilling words: 'This conference is absolutely at an end, and there is no obligation on either side as a result of it.'"[8]

Kruger reportedly left the conference in tears. He had failed, and war appeared inevitable. Milner concluded that some form of military pressure would be needed. Perhaps a military buildup or a show of force: he was not yet thinking about invading the Transvaal. Given the potentially large numbers of Boer fighters and the relatively small number of British forces currently in the Cape Colony, he wanted first to assure himself that British possessions were adequately defended and that reinforcements would soon be forthcoming. Then, perhaps, they could think about more proactive, offensive operations.

Milner framed his thoughts back to London in the form of three key issues presented as questions: how many troops should we have, who will command them, and how far forward should we position our defenses?[9] Milner also had serious doubts about the skills and competence of some of the senior British military commanders. He wanted General Sir William Butler, the commander in chief of the British Army in the Cape Colony, to be removed and communicated this back to London.

Throughout that June, July, and August (winter in the Southern Hemisphere), the Boers offered diluted and marginally revised versions of Bloemfontein proposals. However, their efforts were desultory and not seen as anything serious by Milner or Chamberlain. The last unsatisfactory response from the British was sent to the Boers on

---

[7] Edwards, J., *British History*, (Bell and Hyman Limited: 1981), p.340.
[8] Pakenham, T., *The Boer War*, (Abacus: London 2022), p. 68.
[9] Pakenham, T., *The Boer War*, (Abacus: London 2022), p. 69.

September 8th, 1899.[10] Diplomacy was now officially dead. In September, both sides started to mobilize and reinforce their armies.

White Mans's War

Both sides had a tacit agreement that should a conflict break out, it should remain a "white man's war." No black Africans should be involved in the fighting and should certainly not be armed. Both the British and the Boers greatly feared tribal uprisings. In reality, however, both sides made extensive use of black Africans in a variety of ways. It is a story that is not well researched or known. The British were comfortable arming black Africans in some situations. Colonel Robert Baden-Powell, under siege in Mafeking, created an armed unit entirely of black workers. Black Africans performed a range of military and logistical supporting roles on both sides. The Boers used many as slave labor, forcing them to dig trenches and create other fortifications. African workers acted as guards, laborers, cooks, guides, spies, and mule and oxen drivers. Thousands of black Africans died in the concentration camps alongside the Boer families whom they had been charged with serving.

War Clouds Gather: The Boers Prepare

From October, as the summer campaigning season began to approach, Kruger had some tough and urgent decisions to make. If war was coming, to delay would be to allow the British to pull in thousands of troops from Britain and across its extensive empire and launch an attack in its own good time. Once the British had superior numbers, there would be no ready response. It would be much better, surely, to launch a preemptive strike and try to snatch a quick victory before the might of the British Empire could be brought to bear on them.

Kruger's mind was made up. He worked to ensure that he had President Steyn of the "sister" republic, the Orange Free State, politically and militarily behind him. Technically, the Orange Free State had less of a quarrel with the British. There were no gold or diamond mines, no Uitlanders, and none of the highly charged confrontations seen in Johannesburg. However, the threat to the Boer culture and way of life meant President Steyn and his government had to stand side by side with Kruger. With Steyn on his side, it was Kruger's turn to create an artificial

---

[10] Edwards, J., *British History*, (Bell and Hyman Limited: 1981), p.342.

provocation.

On October 9th, 1899, he sent an ultimatum to the British, giving them forty-eight hours to withdraw all British military forces from the borders of the Transvaal and to pull back any military reinforcements that had been sent to Cape Colony since June 1st. In actuality, there had only been four companies of soldiers (about three or four hundred men) from a Lancashire regiment near the border at the time, but the provocation had the desired impact in London. British sentiments were aroused. Some found it entertaining, but many more found it impudent and insulting that the British Empire could be spoken to in such a way. The mood, fanned by the British press, became more belligerent and supportive of war.

Unsurprisingly, Milner's response was negative. In bland, diplomatic language, the reply committed the two sides to war:

"10th October. – Her Majesty's Government have received with great regret the peremptory demands of the Government of the South African Republic, conveyed in your telegram of the 9th October. You will inform the Government of the South African Republic in reply that the conditions demanded by the Government of the South African Republic are such as her Majesty's Government deem it impossible to discuss."[11]

On October 11th, 1899, war was officially declared. On October 12th, Boer forces from the two republics began an invasion of the Cape Colony and Natal.

---

[11] Doyle, C., *The Great Boer War,*' Sep. 1902, https://www.gutenberg.org/files/3069/3069-h/3069-h.htm

Chapter 4 – The Battlefield And the Opponents

The British and Boer Armies

Before we get into the details of the three-year conflict, we should give ourselves a better sense of the forces involved, including their size, capabilities, weapons, and tactics, and the terrain. Both forces had strengths and weaknesses, and both frequently struggled to understand the other's capabilities and likely actions.

The course of the conflict would surprise and shock both parties. The difficulty in reading the minds of the enemy commanders would lead to some catastrophic blunders and cost many lives. The Boer army did not fit neatly into the categories of armies that the British Army had recently been required to fight. They were not primitive Afghan or African tribesmen, nor were they a large professional continental European army like the Germans, French, or Russians. Many British officers—Redvers Buller in particular—had fought alongside the Boers in some of the tribal wars and had fought against the Boers in the First Boer War of 1880 to 1881. These officers had some appreciation of the culture and qualities of the Boer people and their approach to fighting. However, the British Army as a whole was inadequate in its preparations. The army did not seem to have a concept of operations that would allow them to confront and defeat the Boers.

Here, in a nutshell, was the British problem as they stumbled into this war:

"Despite the great reforms undertaken by Cardwell and Lansdowne's additions to the Army, Britain was not militarily prepared. There was no general staff, no plan of campaign. It was a long time since the Army had had to fight a foe of equal calibre, armed with equal weapons and misleading reports from South Africa had left them ignorant of the fact that the Boers were in this category."[12]

In 1879, in South Africa, over more or less the same climate and terrain—and sometimes even the same battlefields—upon which the British and Boers were to maneuver against each other, the British Army had fought the Zulu Kingdom. Although the powerful British Army, with its artillery, machine guns, and modern rifles, had ultimately crushed King Cetwayo and the Zulu impis, the British capacity for arrogance and underestimation of the enemy had been at the root of some disastrous defeats. At the Battle of Isandlwana, an entire modern field force, well equipped for battle, had been more or less wiped out because of poor planning, poor communications, and a surprise attack by an enemy that the British had considered incapable of such an action.

The British Army was not well suited to anything more than the steady stream of tribal conflicts it encountered while running a global empire. It was not well prepared for confronting soldiers with modern weaponry and mobile tactics. The army was small and scattered. It was weighed down by arcane traditions and run by the intensely inefficient bureaucracy of the War Office.

There were perhaps ten thousand British troops in South Africa before the war broke out.[13] As the War Office and army hurried to put together a larger force to support and reinforce Milner and the field commanders in the Cape, the concept of the larger, centrally structured army they were trying to assemble did not really exist, despite it having been called for.

"Prior to the Anglo-Boer War (1899-1902) the army was not divided into field armies, corps, divisions, or even brigades on a regular basis. The 'division' at Aldershot was not a real division and consisted merely of the troops who happened to be stationed for training there at any one time...The British Army was basically a mere collection of regiments

---

[12] Edwards, J., *British History*, (Bell and Hyman Limited: 1981), p.343.
[13] Pakenham, T., *The Boer War*, (Abacus: London 2022), p. 74.

which were assembled in any order a general saw fit when the need arose."[14]

However, the British Army was at least equipped with all the trappings of a modern army of the time; it had engineers, an advanced logistics system, artillery, cavalry, and machine guns. There was a Royal Army Medical Corps providing, in theory at least, medical attention on the battlefield and hospital units farther back. There was a sophisticated array of observation and communications apparatus, such as balloons, searchlights, heliographs (essentially mirrors reflecting the sun), signaling lamps for nighttime, and telegraph cables allowing (again, in theory) the deployment of field telephones for immediate contact between commanders at the front and generals at the rear.

The Boers had little of this. Estimates vary but suggest that, fully mobilized, the Boers could put a force of approximately forty thousand to fifty thousand fighters into the field.[15] The Boers were predominantly farmers. They owned farmsteads and plots of land that were often very far from major cities. They were brought up from a very early age to hunt animals for food, protect their land and property, and fight off local African tribes when conflicts broke out. Before President Kruger was in his teens, he had witnessed many battles against African tribes and had helped provide ammunition for the adults as the battles played out. As a result, these citizen fighters were all highly skilled in the use of horses and rifles. They went to war dressed in their regular work clothes. They volunteered to take part in the battles and operated as loose groups of independent horsemen. It was a very democratic force. Each fighter thought himself just as good as the commanders and often demanded a say in the planning and execution of military operations. Commanders were elected from amongst the civilians.

The culture of the Boer fighter has been recognized by guerrilla fighters throughout history, particularly by the Afghan tribesmen, who were causing problems in a different part of the British Empire at the time of the Boer War. The Boers preferred to fight and withdraw rather than fight pitched battles or conduct last-ditch stands. The skills they possessed—high mobility and accurate rifles for sniping—suited them well

---

[14] Farwell, B., *Mr. Kipling's Army*, (W. W. Norton and Company: New York, 1981), p.21.

[15] Pakenham, T., *The Boer War*, (Abacus: London 2022), p. 74.

to these "hit-and-run" tactics. This is how Boer War historian Thomas Packenham describes the Boers' set-up and ethos:

"Their elected civilian leaders were made commandants – appointed, that is, to lead the five hundred to two thousand burghers of each commando in battle. In this commando system, it was no one's job to train the burghers. Apart from the annual *wappenschauw* (or shooting practice) the men were left to fight as they had always fought—with the tactics of the mounted frontiersmen. If the enemy were superior in numbers, they would provoke the enemy's attack, dismount, take cover and shoot, remount and ride away."[16]

Weapons, Training, and Tactics

The British Army had good rifles. In 1888, the Lee-Metford had replaced the potent Martini-Henry of Zulu War fame. It was powerful, effective, and had a good range. Despite these qualities, it did not have a long service life. In 1895, the Lee-Enfield was introduced. It was very similar to its predecessor. It had a bolt-action magazine with the same caliber, a .303 inch, or 7.7 millimeter, bullet. The British Army would use both weapons during the campaign.

The Boers were also very comfortable handling these weapons whenever they were captured on the battlefield because the Boers had a very similar and very modern weapon as well. After the Jameson Raid, the Boers bought weapons from Europe, particularly from the Germans and French. The German Mauser rifle was very modern. In 1898, it was adopted by the German Army as its basic infantry weapon. It was also a bolt-action weapon, with a magazine holding five bullets of 7.92mm. The Model 98 Mauser would prove highly successful around the world. Around one hundred million were made between 1898 and 1945. In the hands of the skilled Boer riflemen, they were deadly over long ranges.[17]

The British had evolved their tactics somewhat over the last twenty years. Whereas the army that confronted the Zulus had worn red tunics, the use of khaki uniforms had been regularized and adopted since the 1880s. This allowed the soldiers to blend in with the countryside and present less of a target. Officers were much less likely to be seen

---

[16] Pakenham, T., *The Boer War*, (Abacus: London 2022), p. 105.
[17] Taylor, B., 'The Mauser 98: The Best Bolt-Action Rifle Ever Made?,' *Warfare History Network*, May 2010, https://warfarehistorynetwork.com/article/mauser-98-the-best-bolt-action-rifle-ever-made/

brandishing swords at the front of their troops; they were much more likely to wield a rifle if only to look more like a common soldier and avoid the unwanted attention of a Boer sniper. Similarly, bright metal buttons, shiny epaulets, and medals were removed. The British still advanced on the enemy in highly visible straight lines, although they were now more likely to have spacings of several paces between each man to reduce the impact of a bullet, shell, or machine gun burst. Interestingly, these practices were not standardized; different battalions or brigades might operate in different ways according to the preferences of the individual commander. Some might advance shoulder to shoulder, while others might march as many as fifteen paces apart.

The British were a slow-moving force and dependent upon miles and miles of supply columns, thousands of mules and wagons, dirt tracks, and railway lines. They struggled to respond quickly to an attack and were vulnerable to ambushes. The Boers, on the other hand, could quickly cover large distances across the rolling grasslands known as the veld. They were a highly mobile force. When they were required to stand and fight, they would make excellent use of artillery, as well as spades, pickaxes, and other digging tools to create impressive earthworks, bunkers, and trenches. They moved cautiously in small dispersed groups in dull brown and dusty black work clothing. They sought cover from prying eyes amongst rocks, bushes, and foliage. Their Mauser rifles, machine guns, and artillery used a smokeless form of gunpowder. Gone were the days of the Napoleonic era "fog of war." While this did not entirely remove smoke from the discharge of a weapon and from the battlefield, it certainly made it very hard for British soldiers to identify and shoot at distant targets. The British Army had not fully embraced the concept.[18]

Furthermore, the British had not been that impressed by other game-changing military technologies of the period:

"There was considerable resistance to the machine gun. Hiram S. Maxim, an American, conducted successful field tests of his invention in 1884, but the gun was not adopted. It was thought to be too expensive to use (£5 per minute), and there was some confusion as to whether it should be considered an infantry or artillery weapon. General John

---

[18] Farwell, B., *Mr. Kipling's Army*, (W. W. Norton and Company: New York, 1981), pp.113-114.

Adye, an artillery officer writing in 1894, said that the machine gun 'had not, in my opinion, much future in a campaign against a modern army' and that they 'would add considerably to the impedimenta of troops in the field.'"[19]

The Boer strategy, once war had been declared, was for a speedy, mobile, and decisive attack straight into Natal and the Cape Colony. They wanted to compel the British to come to peace terms before major reinforcements could arrive. For the British, it was imperative to assume a defensive position until reinforcements could land and then push straight to Johannesburg, making use of the crucial railway lines that could support their supply requirements. Both strategies were to come undone almost immediately.

---

[19] Farwell, B., *Mr. Kipling's Army*, (W. W. Norton and Company: New York, 1981), p.114.

Chapter 5 – The First Phase: Boers on the Attack

Boers in a trench during the Second Boer War.
https://commons.wikimedia.org/wiki/File:Mafikeng_Second_Boer_War.jpg

The Boers Strike First

The outer edges of the Cape Colony and Natal territories were of prime concern for the British government, Chamberlain, and Milner once it became clear that the Boers looked likely to strike. Natal, which lay far in the southeast, looked particularly vulnerable, with the large town of Ladysmith within easy reach of the Boers.

Kimberley and Mafeking were in the easternmost part of the Cape Colony. They were also very exposed. Kimberley was the diamond mine capital of the world. It was more or less Cecil Rhodes's town; he had extensive mines and investment interests there. His company dominated public and political affairs, providing employment and even a security force. Rhodes went there to supervise the defenses.

Mafeking was two hundred miles north of Kimberley and was potentially in even greater jeopardy. It was only 150 miles west of the Boer capital, Johannesburg. The defenses of Mafeking would fall to Colonel Robert Baden-Powell, a special service officer who arrived from England in July.[20] No one was sure if the Boers would lay siege to the towns, storm them, or bypass them and press on into the Cape Colony itself.

British Field Force under Redvers Buller

South Africa was in turmoil. Many thousands of Uitlanders and black African workers were now refugees, fleeing west from the Transvaal in anticipation of a conflict. Some Boers in the Cape Colony returned to the Boer republics to fight. British fear of an uprising amongst Cape Colony Boers was a very real and persistent issue. Newly arriving British Empire forces were rushed in the other direction, to the east. The railways and seaborne transportation were under intense strain.

Alfred Milner pressed three issues with London. He wanted competent commanders to be sent, he wanted large numbers of reinforcements, and above all, he wanted a defensible line of positions with which to resist a Boer advance. He faced problems. The bulk of the reinforcements had not yet arrived, but the Boers were already mobilized and likely already moving to attack.

The commander of the British forces in Natal was General George White. He had only recently arrived in the Cape in September and was not yet familiar with the ground. He was a pale-skinned man from Ireland who burned easily in the sun. His bravery was not in dispute. He had won the Victoria Cross, Britain's highest military award for bravery in battle. However, he was entirely unfamiliar with South Africa and the Boers, having spent almost his entire career in India. Out of touch with developments during his sea journey from England, he was alarmed by the reports of Boer advances on his arrival, which were briefed to him by Milner. White abandoned his initial plans for familiarization briefings

---

[20] Baden-Powell would later go on to form the British Boy Scouts movement.

and visits and rushed directly to Natal, barely making his train connection.[21]

One of White's field commanders, Major General Sir William Penn Symons, had, in the absence of specific instructions, used his initiative and taken it upon himself to take a brigade of soldiers—four battalions that numbered approximately four thousand men—and push them well beyond Ladysmith to the small town of Dundee, another forty or so miles to the northeast. Penn Symons had a reputation for impetuosity; in other words, he was a hothead. His unsanctioned advance was a potentially highly risky maneuver; he had divided his forces, thereby weakening them, which military theory states should be avoided at all costs. He also put his small force at risk of being cut off from the main body at Ladysmith.

Back in Aldershot, General Redvers Henry Buller, soon (and briefly) to be in charge of the reinforcements heading to South Africa, was adamant that no British forces should move north of the Tugela River until the initial defensive phase of the operation had been completed. The river offered the greatest hope for an effective defense of Natal. Penn Symons was well beyond the Tugela. He was jeopardizing the entire eastern front.[22]

In Britain, General Buller was frantically trying to organize a corps of three divisions, which would become the Natal Field Force, to come to the aid of the Cape Colony. Telegrams had gone out to all corners of the empire. Soldiers were being sent from India, Egypt, Malta, and Crete.

Buller was a veteran of campaigns in South Africa and had fought the Zulus in 1879, where he had won the Victoria Cross. He had fought alongside the Boers in this campaign and against the Boers during the First Boer War in 1881. He had a good understanding of their culture and an appreciation of their fighting capabilities. Some of the chattering classes in London suggested that Buller was perhaps too supportive of the Boers and were concerned that perhaps he admired them a little too much. However, he was very popular with the public and with his soldiers, who admired his open and genuine concern for the well-being of the common soldier. But Buller had weaknesses. He was an

---

[21] Pakenham, T., *The Boer War*, (Abacus: London 2022), p. 99.
[22] Pakenham, T., *The Boer War*, (Abacus: London 2022), p. 107.

indecisive micro-manager who was prone to panic attacks.

Early Boer Successes

On October 12th, 1899, the telegraph connection to Mafeking went dead. The first military action of the Boer War took place on October 12th when a force of Boers under Koos de la Rey attacked a small British garrison at a set of railway sidings midway between Mafeking and Vryburg. The British force surrendered after a five-hour fight. The Boers destroyed an armored train and captured many supplies and much ammunition.

On October 14th, contact was lost with Kimberley. Kimberley and Mafeking were both now effectively in a state of siege. The British started to receive reports that the senior Boer commander (and previous vice president to Kruger), Piet Joubert, was advancing south toward Natal, slowly winding through the passes of the Drakensberg and Biggarsberg mountains with a large Boer force.

In the early morning of October 20th, the British force under Penn Symons at Dundee had just fallen out after a parade. The main camp, consisting of rows of tents, was one mile to the west of the town. In the mist, drizzle, and gloom, the British were in full battle dress and anticipating breakfast followed by a full day of combat training. Penn Symons's force, which included cavalry, did not appear to have put scouts out to any significant degree. The British had not identified where the main Boer force was, which perhaps explains why what happened next came as a bit of a surprise.

Talana Hill and Elandslaagte

To the east of Dundee stood the hill of Talana. The Boer threat was broadly expected to be coming in from the north, behind Impati Mountain, later rather than sooner. That morning, someone noticed a group of men moving on the top of Talana Hill. When binoculars were brought to bear, the group appeared to be armed Boers, some of whom were clustered around artillery pieces. This was a strike force from Lucas Meyer's commando unit, which was part of Joubert's drive south.

The Creusot 75mm guns opened fire with sharp cracks that echoed over the town. The British soldiers were confused, and the officers were momentarily paralyzed. A chaotic rush followed, as men grabbed their weapons, saddled horses, and prepared for battle. These soldiers, which included a battalion of the 60th Rifles, the regiment that had seen an ignominious defeat at the infamous Battle of Majuba in 1881, had never faced hostile artillery. Many of the soldiers had not yet seen combat.

Luckily, the Boer artillery bombardment only amounted to three guns firing sporadically and inaccurately. There were next to no casualties, barring one officer's horse that was blown to pieces by a direct hit and a bugler boy who had his head taken off by a shell. As the South African Boer War historian Des Latham would dryly observe, "The Boers weren't much good at artillery initially. They would get better."[23]

The British scrambled to prepare for the first action of the campaign. Royal Artillery gunners sweated and heaved as they struggled to drag their eighteen field artillery pieces into place to bombard Talana Hill. General Penn Symons dictated his orders from the comfort of his tent, bemoaning the sheer impudence of the Boers for daring to start the war before he had finished his breakfast.

Symons's battle plan was simple and lifted straight from the pages of the Aldershot training manual. A brisk artillery barrage would pin and pummel the Boers on the hill. His infantry would engage in a frontal attack straight up the hill. Then, his cavalry force, the 18th Hussars under Lieutenant Colonel Möller, would sweep around the flank and rear of the retreating Boers and cut them off.[24]

By now, intelligence reports were coming in of another tentacle of Joubert's forces approaching from behind Impati Mountain. Time was short.

But Symons's plans had a significant flaw. Symons still favored a close concentration of men for an infantry attack—an old school "shoulder to shoulder" approach, where guts and verve would carry the day.

While the British artillery pounded Talana, three of the infantry battalions lined themselves along a dry river at the foot of the hill. The fourth battalion had been kept back at the camp with one of the artillery batteries. At the very least, Symons understood there was a risk of a flank attack by one of Joubert's forces.

The infantry made ready for their part in the attack. Colonel Bobby Gunning of the 60th Rifles encouraged the soldiers to remember and avenge Majuba.

---

[23] Latham, D., The Anglo-Boer War podcast, episode five, https://www.abwarpodcast.com/
[24] Pakenham, T., *The Boer War*, (Abacus: London 2022), p. 128.

The inexperienced infantry rose to their feet and surged forward. They were immediately met by accurate fire. The lines of soldiers soon broke apart into smaller, less organized groups of soldiers. They took shelter behind trees, bushes, and the walls and ditch of a farm at the base of the hill. The forward momentum was slow. It was still drizzling.

Impatient for news that the hill had been taken, General Symons rode forward on his horse to see what the problem was and to set an example for his men. The brigade commander wanted to postpone the attack and let the artillery take more time to hit the Boer positions. Symons refused. He got off his horse and walked to the front line, a wall with gaps in it behind which huddled some of the British infantry. He walked beyond the wall and shortly returned, apparently in great discomfort. He got back on his horse and slowly rode back down the hill. Out of sight, he allowed his staff to take him off the horse and place him on a stretcher. He had been badly wounded in the stomach and would die the next day.[25]

The British infantry slowly fought their way to the top of the hill, fixing bayonets once they got close enough for a final charge. In the last attack of the battle (the Boers showing no desire to stand and face bayonets), a British artillery battery in Dundee, unsure of who was friendly and who was enemy, fired on British soldiers near the summit, killing and wounding many.

The 18th Hussars and some mounted infantry headed off around both sides of Talana Hill to try and exploit the win, but their efforts were fruitless. The Boers had made a smart exit. Ironically, the British artillery had spotted men moving eastward on horseback but had mistaken them for British cavalry and had not opened fire.

So, the British, technically at least, could claim a victory. They had taken the hill, and the Boers had fled the field of battle. But the cost had been high. Symons lay in a hospital tent, dying. Several other officers lay dead, including Colonel Gunning of the 60th Rifles, or dying. One officer had lost both legs to a bursting British shrapnel shell. In all, the British suffered fifty killed and two hundred wounded. The Boers had lost twenty-three killed, sixty-six wounded, and twenty captured. The Boers had demonstrated determination in resisting the British attack.

---

[25] Pakenham, T., *The Boer War*, (Abacus: London 2022), p. 130.

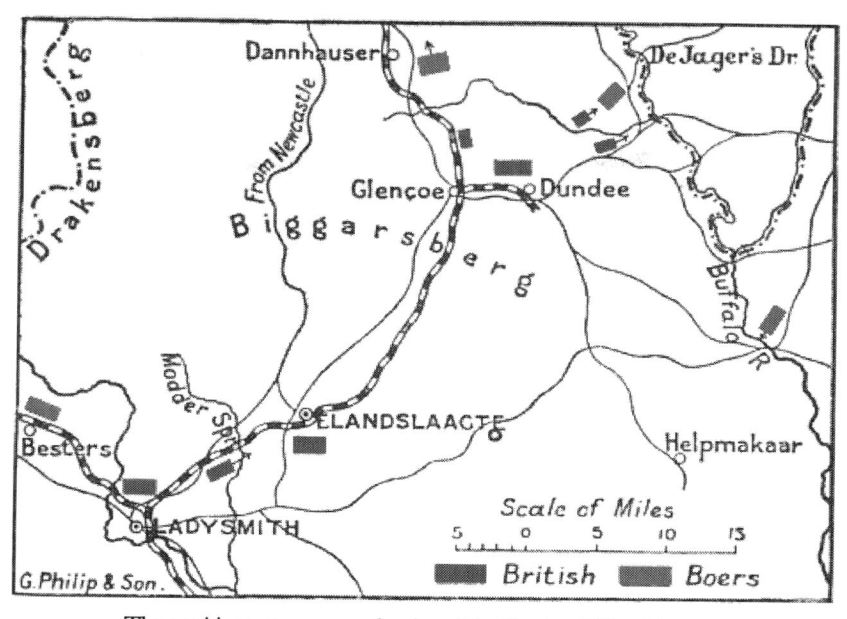

The positions at noon on the day of the Battle of Elandslaagte.
https://commons.wikimedia.org/wiki/File:Battle_of_Elandslaagte_Map.png

The next day, closer to Ladysmith, farther south down the railway line, news emerged that other Boer forces were threatening to cut off the Dundee garrison. Forces under General Johannes Kock had taken control of the railway station there, severing the rail and telegraph connections between Ladysmith and Dundee. It also meant that Boer commandos were now only fourteen miles from Ladysmith.

General White sent a cavalry force under Major General John French to investigate. French confirmed the station was in enemy hands and came under fire from two Boer artillery pieces. He retired hastily and reported back to White, who sent French back to Elandslaagte, along with an infantry brigade of four battalions under Colonel Ian Hamilton.

The Boers, who had around one thousand men and three artillery pieces, positioned themselves on a ridge overlooking the railway. This time, the British approach was slightly more creative, although it was not dissimilar to Penn Symons's approach at Talana Hill. Colonel Hamilton favored the troops advancing in open order, with three yards between each man, so they were slightly less vulnerable to the Boer marksmen.

Under the intense gaze of journalists from four London newspapers, the attack commenced. After an artillery barrage, one battalion, the 1st Devons, made a frontal attack, while the other three battalions made an attack around the right flank. French's cavalry pushed around both flanks, again looking to try and cut off the Boers. The attack was successful; the infantry moved to the bottom of the hill and, despite heavy fire, attacked up it.

A rainstorm suddenly reduced visibility, and they were hampered by barbed wire fences across the farmland. As they successfully advanced to the top of the ridge, the Boers retreated down the rear of the hill and began to mount their horses. In the confusion, a Boer raised a white flag on one part of the hill, and some British troops stopped to take the surrender. At the same time, the Boer commander, General Johannes Kock, an old man wearing a black coat and a top hat, led an unsuccessful counterattack. Kock was wounded and captured, dying of his injuries in a British hospital a few days later. The Boers escaping on horseback were caught by the British cavalry, and many were killed by swords and lances. A large part of the British cavalry was mistakenly sent around Impati Mountain, where they were ineffective for most of the battle.

This was another British victory, although it came at a high cost. The Boers lost 350 fighters and their commander and quit the field. The British lost 35 officers and 202 men; this was a high rate of officer loss and was likely a result of the Boers deliberately singling them out to hamper the effectiveness of the command and control of the infantry forces.[26] The win on the battlefield was shortly be made redundant, as the Dundee garrison would abandon the town within hours.

More intelligence reports came to General White, back in Ladysmith, suggesting that Joubert was nearing Ladysmith with a force as large as ten thousand fighters (in reality, it was probably near six thousand, and White's command had around eight thousand). He sent word to the forces at Elandslaagte and Dundee that they should fall back to Ladysmith immediately. They did this, but the movement of the forces at Dundee, having lost so many officers and being bombarded sporadically by Boer heavy artillery since Talana Hill, deteriorated into something of a panic, fearing they would be cut off. They abandoned massive stocks of supplies and equipment. They left in a disorganized and demoralized state, unnecessarily fearful of being caught by the Boers as they retreated. The field hospital, its staff, and the wounded were

---

[26] 'Battle of Elandslaagte, *Great Boer War*, https://www.britishbattles.com/great-boer-war/battle-of-elandslaagte/

surrendered to the Boers, who treated them well. Poor General Penn Symons was left to die of his wounds under the respectful gaze of the Boer captors.

Chapter 6 – Relieving the Sieges: Kimberley, Ladysmith, and Mafeking

Ladysmith was not yet surrounded, but the situation was growing increasingly serious. All that the forward positions at Dundee and Elandslaagte and the two battles had achieved was to demonstrate that Buller had been correct in advocating staying south of the Tugela. The problem now was with General White. At sixty-four, he was rather old for an active and stressful military command. He did not understand the Boers and did not know what to do with their highly mobile forces. Commandos were closing in from the north and west. While Buller was still pushing for a withdrawal back to the Tugela, the British governor of Natal, Hely-Hutchinson, did not want to cede any more British territory than necessary. White's force was supposed to be defending Natal. Now, it looked as if he would be the one needing help.

The clock was ticking. The Ladysmith water supplies had already been cut off. As White surveyed the situation, he looked anxiously for a Boer target that he could strike and defeat, hoping, even at this stage, to be able to restore some balance to the military situation. As he dithered, Boer guns were being maneuvered onto Pepworth Hill, bringing them into range of the Ladysmith garrison. White seized on this. He had found his target. Or had he? He would use the word "hoped" in his description of the enemy locations.[27] And "hope" is rarely a solid part of a good plan.

Against much advice, he settled on a complicated night maneuver, using both his infantry brigades, one of which was expected to find its way through enemy lines and position itself in the rear of the Boers. White's and the British military system's weaknesses are described by Thomas Packenham:

"What if the Boers, all mounted and hence exceptionally mobile, decided not to provide the objective in the place he hoped? His plan did not allow any flexibility. It was like a series of chess moves devised without any regard for the moves of an opponent. And if the plan failed, two British brigades would be forced to improvise one. They would be thrown back on their own resources—a situation for which neither officers nor men had yet shown any great aptitude. Yet this was not the feature of White's plan that alarmed his staff officers most. What gave it an air of absolute recklessness was that White proposed to send a second column on a night march through the enemy lines."[28]

Night navigation is always difficult, particularly for inexperienced troops with limited knowledge of either the plan or the terrain. After a brief skirmish with Boer horsemen, a large part of the mule column carrying vital artillery and ammunition bolted off in the darkness. The men of the Gloucestershire Battalion arrived at where they thought they were meant to be. When dawn broke, they found themselves on a plateau overlooked by Boer troops on surrounding higher peaks. In the resulting firefight, the British ran out of ammunition quickly, having lost their mules. At two o'clock that afternoon, the force surrendered to the Boers.

The other flank attack, under Colonel Geoffrey Grimwood, fared little better. The Boers were not where they were supposed to be. Some of Grimwood's guns had gone missing, and the cavalry units were in the wrong place. The British soldiers continued to suffer heavily from Boer gunfire.

---

[27] Pakenham, T., *The Boer War*, (Abacus: London 2022), p. 152.
[28] Pakenham, T., *The Boer War*, (Abacus: London 2022), p. 152.

Boer artillery started firing at Ladysmith itself. White recalled the soldiers, who moved back under continuous fire. About one thousand British soldiers were taken prisoner, and there was a total of 1,400 losses.[29] It was a humiliation for General White and the British Army. White rightly took full responsibility for the plan's failure. Both Buller and London privately agreed that White should be sacked (he actually ended up a field marshal), but in the absence of any realistic alternatives, he remained in command of the Ladysmith garrison until it was relieved.

Ladysmith was far from an ideal location to defend under siege. It was on low ground and surrounded on all sides by hills and ridges—an ideal place for enemy artillery positions and observers to dominate the battlefield.

Mafeking, under the command of Baden-Powell, was also surrounded by Boer forces. Baden-Powell had secretly begun training mounted horsemen in August 1899 and building defenses in and around the town in September. He could muster around two thousand soldiers to defend the town.

The telegraph cables were cut on October 12th, and Boer artillery began shelling after Mafeking refused an offer to surrender. Baden-Powell was proactive and energetic in his approach to the defense of Mafeking, constructing trenches and defensive positions. It was to be a long siege.

It would also be a long siege for Kimberley. Cecil Rhodes's "Diamond City" had electric street lighting even before London did. The city was encircled shortly after Mafeking was besieged. The British military commander was Colonel Robert Kekewich. He had half a battalion of British infantry, a handful of guns and machine guns, and two thousand irregular troops. Although the city had been at risk from the Boers for some months, it was not prepared for a long siege.

Cecil Rhodes was determined to get into Kimberley to monitor and protect his investments despite many citizens' efforts to discourage him. Once in the town, he made a total nuisance of himself, controlling large parts of the community and the security forces. He would greatly undermine and sometimes directly challenge Kekewich's military

---

[29] 'The battle of Ladysmith,' *Great Boer War*, https://www.britishbattles.com/great-boer-war/battle-of-ladysmith/

leadership, as he continually sent private messages back to Milner and the Cape Colony, demanding that Kimberley be relieved urgently and at all costs.

Not all the Boer leaders were convinced that laying siege to the three towns was a good idea. Some felt it was a waste of the Boers' exceptional mobility, and others felt the towns should have been quickly stormed before the British got a chance to fully dig themselves in.

General Joubert was old and not particularly dynamic. At Ladysmith, he summoned his commanders for a discussion and to take a vote on how to deal with the town. Some wanted to drive south to the coast and seize the crucial ports. However, the vote was in favor of a siege.

During this early period of the conflict, the Boer leadership showed a distinct lack of top-level strategy, with little plan other than to protect their own republics and little desire for conquest of British territories, which was London's and the Cape Colony's biggest fear.

Buller's Siege Dilemma

Redvers Buller left Southampton dock on October 14th. Military staff and many journalists accompanied him, including an ambitious twenty-five-year-old called Winston Churchill, who was still technically an army officer but temporarily detached from his regiment and acted in the capacity of a journalist for *The Morning Post*. On the ship, they were cut off from all outside communications. Speculation was rife about the likely state of the Boer situation. In late October, a couple of days before they reached Cape Town, a tramp steamer was traveling in the opposite direction, away from South Africa. It passed close by them. Churchill records:

"As a bold half-measure, signals were made to the steamer, asking for news. On this she altered her course and steamed past us a little more than a hundred yards distant ... A blackboard was held up from the deck of the tramp, and on this we read the following legend:

BOERS DEFEATED
THREE BATTLES
PENN SYMONS KILLED

Then she faded away behind us and we were left to meditate upon this cryptic message."[30]

Churchill was unimpressed. He felt they could have spent a little bit more time gathering some useful information from the departing steamer. Ironically, within a couple of weeks, Churchill himself was to make news. He would be captured by the Boers on the Ladysmith front when the armored train he was in was derailed by a Boer ambush.

Upon Buller's arrival in Cape Town, he was immediately under pressure from all directions. What should he do? In theory, his mission was to take his three-division army corps and advance it northeast, straight up the railway, to take Johannesburg and Pretoria. Milner, however, was worried about a general pro-Boer uprising in the Cape Colony and wanted Buller to stay to protect against any unrest or uprising. Kimberley, Ladysmith, and Mafeking were under siege, pinning down large numbers of British soldiers. They had limited food supplies, although the situation was not yet critical for any of the towns. But in Kimberley, Rhodes's high-pitched pleadings were a form of emotional blackmail. He began to hint that he might surrender the town if no one came to its aid.

Buller, who was not known for his decisiveness, pondered, took advice, and formulated his plan. He decided to divide his corps into three different-sized detachments to relieve the three besieged towns. This meant there would be no decisive advance on the Boer capital any time soon. It also meant a logistical nightmare for Buller and the troops, who were arriving piecemeal on different troop ships and being sent to different ports according to a timetable that was now out of date and to a plan that was being dramatically reworked.

The three divisions were to be sent in different directions. The 1st Division would be under Lieutenant General Lord Methuen, who was charged with moving north and relieving Ladysmith and then Mafeking. Major General Francis Clery commanded the 2nd Division, two brigades of which would form a protective screen around Pietermaritzburg against further Boer incursions past Ladysmith and deeper into Natal. Lieutenant General William Forbes Gatacre commanded the 3rd

---

[30] Churchill, W., My Early Life, A Roving Commission (R. Maclehose and Co.: London 1944), pp. 249-250.

Division, but he had a much smaller group of three thousand soldiers. He was to hold the railway junction at Stormberg on the southern border of the Orange Free State to guard against Boer incursions and local unrest. Redvers Buller would take the remainder of the corps and prepare to liberate Ladysmith.

General Methuen went into action first, so we shall start by following the progress of the 1st Division and the efforts to relieve Kimberley. The mission appeared straightforward—or so Buller and Methuen thought. Methuen was to take his ten-thousand-man force, cross the Orange River, brush aside the Boers, and travel seventy-five miles to relieve Kimberley. The route would follow the railway, allowing for necessary supplies and reinforcements to support the comprehensive but cumbersome British logistical process.

Belmont, Graspan, and Modder River

One of the challenges that was emerging for the British during the early stages of the efforts to relieve Kimberley, Ladysmith, and Mafeking was that the Boers made it very difficult for scouts on horseback to get too close. Boer marksmanship with the modern Mauser rifles made it very dangerous for the British cavalry screen to get too close. This meant that British commanders frequently had a poor understanding of where the Boers were, in what numbers, and what defenses they were preparing.

Methuen had a powerful force as he advanced northeast along the railway line to Kimberley. He had the Guards Brigade, comprising four battalions, and the 9th Infantry Brigade, which was of a similar size. There was also a naval brigade made up of marines and infantry, as well as cavalry of the 9th Lancers and sixteen artillery pieces (two full batteries). Methuen would discover that he did not have enough cavalry for the entire range of screening, reconnaissance, and outflanking maneuvers that he needed to support the advance.

By the military standards of the day, Methuen was relatively young at fifty-four. He was the youngest lieutenant general in the British Army. He had absorbed some of the lessons of this theater of war and of this opponent. Methuen insisted that when soldiers approached the enemy, they should be at in extreme extended order, meaning there should be great distances between soldiers. No shiny metal buttons, insignia, epaulets, or swords would be displayed to catch the sun.[31]

Striking camp at dawn on November 21st, reports reached Methuen of a force of perhaps two thousand Boers dug in on a series of hilltops and low mountains just east of the small railway station and the hamlet of Belmont. The intelligence information regarding enemy positions and the terrain was sketchy. Methuen initially wanted to make a large flanking maneuver, but his limited cavalry and his fear of having the railway line cut reduced his options. Furthermore, he had poor-quality maps, and the compasses were affected by the high density of iron in the rocky ground. He decided upon a frontal attack.[32] He also decided that the approach to the Boer positions should be made at night in order to get as close as possible before the Boers could bring their high-quality marksmanship into play.

A few miles south of Belmont station, at around 2:00 a.m. on the morning of November 23rd, the 1st Division set off, having left the camp fires burning in the hope that this might convince the Boers the force was still asleep.

Navigating at night is always problematic. Methuen's inexperienced force only had one chance to practice it together since they had arrived in South Africa, and it had been something of a disaster. The approach started to go awry. As dawn neared, it became clear that the forces were not yet in position and were advancing on the wrong hills. The effort to outflank the Boers was already failing. With little option but to make the best of the situation, the Guards Brigade stormed the hills. The 9th Brigade, on the left of the Guards Brigade, followed suit shortly afterward.

As the battalions got closer to the Boers, they began to lose their bearings, and some battalions attacked the wrong objectives. A problem that many British commanders faced during the Boer War was that hills, ridges, mountains, and other high ground could look very different when viewed from different perspectives, directions, or altitudes. Nevertheless, the hills were eventually cleared after the British faced intense firepower and suffered many casualties. Before the crests fell to the British and their bayonets, the Boers had already retreated down the reverse slope

---

[31] Pemberton, W., *Battles of the Boer War*, (Pan Books, Ltd.: London, 1969), pp.37-38.
[32] Pemberton, W., *Battles of the Boer War*, (Pan Books, Ltd.: London, 1969), p.41.

of the hill, mounted their horses, and began to ride away.

The British cavalry had again been unable to successfully cut off the Boers. The 850 mounted men of the 9th Lancers were inadequate for the tasks they were supposed to perform. What is more, the horses were still weak from the long journey by sea. They had been rushed straight out to the front, so they were weak and regularly went without water. The cavalry regiments rarely had enough horses to fully equip their riders.

It was another "technical victory" for the British; they had stormed a hill, and the Boers had retreated. The British suffered seventy-five killed and two hundred wounded. The Boers might have lost around one hundred, but they had done their job of slowing the British down and delaying the relief of Ladysmith.

Methuen and the British soldiers were reasonably happy with their performance. Most of these soldiers had not been in action before and had had little time to acclimate to the environment and the climate, let alone the fighting potential and tactics of the Boers. However, their satisfaction with the operation was at risk of making them overconfident.[33]

The division pressed on the next day. Eleven miles later, the British approached a railway siding at Graspan. Two miles ahead, the Boers were digging in on hilltops to the east of the railway, and another four miles beyond the high ground lay the railway station of Enslin (the name the Boers gave to the battle).

The battle resembled a smaller version of Belmont. However, the heights were not so dominant, offering a less challenging obstacle. Methuen's intelligence reports indicated four hundred Boer soldiers and two guns. But, again, this reporting turned out to be flawed. It might have been correct at the time, but by the evening of November 24th, another two thousand Boer fighters arrived.

Methuen's artillery barrage began to fire on the morning of November 25th. Boer guns speedily replied, and Methuen suddenly understood that the Boers' position was better defended than previously suspected. He hastily rearranged his plan. The clever flanking maneuvers would be replaced with a more conventional frontal attack. The Naval Brigade carried the day, and the Boers withdrew.

---

[33] Pemberton, W., *Battles of the Boer War*, (Pan Books, Ltd.: London, 1969), p.51.

Yet again, the British cavalry was unable to effectively pursue the retreating Boers. They were too few, and the horses were too tired. Almost half of the horses were unfit. Methuen was again frustrated and removed the commander of the 9th Lancers, Colonel Gough, of his command.[34]

Battle of Modder River

A British illustration of the Battle of Modder River.
https://commons.wikimedia.org/wiki/File:Battle_of_Modder_River_-_Bacon%27s_South_Africa_War_Prints.jpg

The next day, November 26th, the troops rested and reorganized themselves. On November 27th, they moved off, edging ever closer to their goal. Fifteen miles ahead lay the next significant obstacle for Methuen and his division: the railway bridge across the Modder River. This had the potential to be a major defensive position for the Boers.

And it was. The Boers had blown up the bridge. However, the terrain was different this time. There were no major pieces of high ground or kops, meaning there were no significant hills, ridges, or mountains. Houses, farms, and bungalows dotted the area of Rosmead village to the

---

[34] "9th Lancers," British Empire website, https://www.britishempire.co.uk/forces/9thlancers.htm

west of the bridge. The approaches to and from the river were flat, barren scrubland. But green foliage—poplar and eucalyptus trees and bushes—was abundant along the Riet and Modder River lines, making visibility difficult. However, it looked pleasant and peaceful. Some British officers drew comparisons with Maidenhead or Henley. Methuen and his officers planned to take breakfast under the shade of those trees once the Boers had been driven off.

The Boers' tactics were evolving after their encounters with the British. They understood that the British artillery could be very effective and accurate and that it was invariably used to bombard hilltops before a British advance. Although a position on high ground offered advantages of height and range to the Boer riflemen, one of the more effective Boer commanders, Koos de la Ray, noticed that riflemen firing down on targets from a great height were less effective against a large mass of British infantry than firing on flat ground in front of a hill. If a Boer rifleman missed his target on a flat surface, there was still a reasonable chance that he might hit a man (or two) who were advancing behind.

The Boers dug many trenches along the river. They concealed them carefully and cleverly with bushes, grass, and branches. Furthermore, the Boers placed large stones that were painted white outward from the trenches at hundred-yard intervals so they could have an accurate sense of the range they would be firing at as the British approached. The Boers would have a clear field of view as the British came. The Boers would be dispersed in concealed trenches and firing smokeless ammunition, so the British would not be able to see the Boers until they were very close. And, of course, at that point, it would be far too late.[35]

A German Army officer, Major Albrecht, was in charge of the Boer artillery. He arranged for gun pits to be dug amid the trenches to allow him to move his guns to a protected position if needed.

Methuen's plan was hampered by the same problems he had experienced at Belmont and Graspan. His reconnaissance was limited, as the Boer long-range marksmen made it almost impossible to draw near to observe the Boer positions. The maps were entirely inadequate. The Royal Engineers had managed to conduct a hasty investigation of the Boer defenses and produced a quick sketch of their findings. This

---

[35] Pemberton, W., *Battles of the Boer War*, (Pan Books, Ltd.: London, 1969), p.58.

was to become a major problem. The map was very inaccurate. Specifically the location and direction of the Riet River. This caused many casualties for the British.

Another glaring error was that the British were unaware that Bosman's Drift, about four miles down the river to the east, offered a straightforward way to cross. It was something that was a concern to the Boers, who certainly knew of the drift. Although they had strong defenses by the bridge, they were thinly stretched along the river in both directions.

Methuen was unclear about the best approach. He once again considered a flank attack, but he had limited numbers of cavalry, and taking his soldiers on a wide forced march across the baking heat of the veld risked separating him from the railway and his supplies. Reports also told him that the Boers were digging trenches along the river line in front of him, but the Boer numbers were not believed to be great. Other reports suggested that the Boers did not plan to make a strong stand there but that they might be retreating soon to new positions at Spytfontein, closer to Kimberley.

Again, Methuen planned for a flank attack but changed his mind at the last minute and settled on a frontal assault. The 9th Brigade, under General Reginald Pole-Carew, would advance left of the railway line, and the Guards Brigade would be on the right. Methuen thought it likely there were only a few Boers in place—a few hundred at the most.[36]

By the time the British attack went in, however, the Boers were well dug in and numbered somewhere between four and eight thousand fighters.

At 4:30 in the morning of November 28th, both brigades moved forward. The soldiers were confident and were not expecting strong opposition. At 5:15, the Lancers on the flanks received some rifle fire, the first action of the day. They reported this to Methuen, who was dismissive. The soldiers reached a rise and began the gentle three-mile slope downward to the river.

When they were within a mile of the river, Methuen and his staff carefully scanned the line of trees that dotted the river. They could see no sign of the enemy and concluded that the Boers had left. Methuen

---

[36] Pemberton, W., *Battles of the Boer War*, (Pan Books, Ltd.: London, 1969), p.60.

turned his attention to the houses by the riverbank, intent on selecting a comfortable base for his headquarters.

As the forward lines of soldiers got to within half a mile of the river, an intense volume of rifle fire burst out all along the riverbank. Both brigades flung themselves to the ground, and the advance stopped in confusion. Pole-Carew's brigade came under fire from the front and also from farm buildings and rocks to the west. They were being shot at in the flank.

The Guards Brigade attempted to regain some momentum, extending to their right—the east—to try and threaten the Boers' left flank. However, they suddenly found themselves up against a whole river line—the Riet River, which runs north/south—that they did not know was there. Although some soldiers tried to wade and swim across, this major water feature effectively halted their movement.

Both brigades—eight thousand men or so—were largely static throughout the morning, desperately trying to find some shelter amidst the scrub and rocks. As the sun rose, sunstroke, heat exhaustion, aggressive ants, and dehydration became problems. Some soldiers fell asleep after their early morning exertions. The accuracy of the Boer snipers meant that the slightest move of a hand or a helmet could draw instant and accurate fire.[37]

The British soldiers were so hard-pressed for protective cover that they lay flat under the hot baking sun. The Scotsmen in their kilts received terrible blisters on the backs of their knees. For all the soldiers, bullet wounds in the heels or buttocks were commonplace.

In the early afternoon (remembering that, by then, the soldiers had been up and active for almost twelve hours), Pole-Carew got lucky on the left flank. He noticed a gap in the Boer line between the farm on the left flank, which had been giving them so much trouble, and a small clump of trees offering shelter on the riverbank. He pushed some troops quickly forward. Soon, the troops were fording the river by Rosmead village. The Boers on the farm on the south side disappeared. Soon after, the Boers on the north side—the Boers' right flank—started to pull back. The Boer flank was rapidly crumbling.

---

[37] Doyle, C., 'The Great Boer War,' Chapter 8, Lord Methuen's Advance, Sep. 1902, https://www.gutenberg.org/files/3069/3069-h/3069-h.htm

Pole-Carew reported back to Methuen with urgent calls for reinforcements for what appeared to be a significant breakthrough. Nothing came. There was more delay and stagnation. The British and Boer artillery engaged in a protracted duel. British shells landed on Pole-Carew's troops, which dampened their energy for a resumed attack northward.

"Driven back by British as well as Boer fire, Pole-Carew had the mortification of learning later how near he had been to converting a simple victory into a decisive victory. Instead of being able to pursue an enemy, still further demoralised by artillery, following then as they fell back, he had had two hours of scrappy, profitless fighting amongst the trees and gardens and cactus hedges of the north bank and then had to retreat on Rosmead."[38]

There was no further significant movement on the ground by the British that day. As night followed dusk, there was little understanding on the British side as to what was going on; they did not even know who had won or lost. The next morning, the British were able to cross the river unopposed. The Boers had abandoned their positions overnight and completed an orderly withdrawal to their next fighting position with their forces intact.

"No whine of bullet or crash of shell was heard. Where the Boers had been lying in their trenches were to be found nothing but spent cartridge cases and empty bottles of gin. The Boers had gone in the night, as well as their guns."[39]

The Battle of Modder River had been a costly affair for the British. It had been poorly planned and executed by Methuen. His reconnaissance and intelligence efforts had been entirely inadequate. He had been planning and operating more or less blind, with little knowledge of what lay on his flanks. The Boers were already learning to expect British frontal attacks. Piet Cronje, the overall Boer commander, stated, "The English do not make turning movements. They never leave the railway, because they cannot march."[40]

---

[38] Pemberton, W., *Battles of the Boer War*, (Pan Books, Ltd.: London, 1969), p.72.
[39] Pemberton, W., *Battles of the Boer War*, (Pan Books, Ltd.: London, 1969), p.73.
[40] Pemberton, W., *Battles of the Boer War*, (Pan Books, Ltd.: London, 1969), p.59.

Cronje had nearly been wrong. And his force did not come away unscathed; the Boers suffered around sixty dead and three hundred wounded. The British lost one hundred men and nearly four hundred wounded.[41]

On such a brutal battlefield, there were, of course, hundreds of personal tragedies. The Boer commander, Koos de la Rey, lost one of his two teenage sons in this battle. De la Rey was grief-stricken. He left the battlefield and disappeared for several days to bury his son and come to terms with the tragedy. He returned to the troops on the front line later, and he was more bitter and more determined than ever to push the British off his land.

General Methuen suffered as well. He was wounded in the thigh and was evacuated to a field hospital. It was a painful wound, but it was not serious, and he would return to take command later. Methuen's senior staff officer, Lieutenant Colonel Henry Northcott, a close personal friend, was also taken to the hospital. Northcott succumbed to his wounds in the hospital.[42]

"Black Week": Stormberg, Magersfontein, and Colenso

"Black Week" was so named by the British press because the British forces in South Africa suffered three serious defeats in the same week on three different fronts: Magersfontein in the east, Stormberg in the center, and Colenso in the southeast. Although chronologically a little out of alignment, we will first cover Magersfontein since it follows up on Methuen's poor performance at the Battle of Modder River.

Once the Modder River had been cleared of Boers, the British were able to recover and regroup. Horses and men alike were finally able to quench their thirsts. The men also bathed and washed their clothes, even though "Modder" means "muddy" in Afrikaans. There were also numerous human and animal bodies floating downstream, so it was certainly not hygienic. Dysentery and other waterborne diseases posed significant problems in the campaign.

Methuen's troops needed time to reorganize and take on supplies and reinforcements coming up the railway line. There would be no

---

[41] "Battle of Modder River," *Great Boer War*, https://www.britishbattles.com/great-boer-war/battle-of-modder-river/

[42] Pakenham, T., *The Boer War*, (Abacus: London 2022), p. 198.

immediate move forward.

The next obvious defensive position for the Boers was the ridge at Magersfontein, some six miles farther up the railway line toward Kimberley. A Boer council of war intensely debated whether Magersfontein should be defended (this approach was favored by Koos de la Rey and the Transvaal Boers) or whether they should retreat farther back to Spytfontein, which was three miles back (this approach was favored by Piet Cronje and the Orange Free State fighters).

De la Rey actually missed the council meeting, as he was burying his son, but he returned late to convince Cronje that Magersfontein offered the best defensive option. De la Rey was determined that the trenches should be extensive.

Methuen's cavalry patrols did not get close, but it was very clear that the Boers were digging in, once again, for a serious battle. As an indication of the speed and initiative of the Boer commandos and the fragility of the British railway links, on the night of December 6th, Boer troops raided the Enslin station, which was some miles back behind the British lines.

The Boers, sensing a likely frontal British attack, developed an elaborate trench system. Parts of it had barbed wire fences with tin cans tied to the wire in order to give a noisy warning of approaching soldiers. Those Boers with the older Martini-Henry rifles that spurted smoke when fired were put on the ridges looking down. The smokeless Mauser rifle-armed troops were put into the trenches on the ground.

The Boer commanders were keen to convince the British that the real target lay on the hilltops. Reinforcements had come in from the Boer soldiers besieging Ladysmith and also from Natal. By the time of the British attack, there were approximately ten thousand Boer fighters in the defensive system.

Methuen received supplies and reinforcements from the railway line. He got the Highland Brigade—four battalions of Scottish troops under General Adrian Wauchope—another cavalry unit, the 12th Lancers, and three more artillery batteries. In addition, he got a tethered balloon for aerial reconnaissance; it was equipped with a telephone cable to report an overview of the battle. Methuen had around twelve thousand troops.

His plan of attack bore all the trappings of Belmont, Graspan, and Modder River. After a two-hour artillery barrage, the fresh troops of the Highland Brigade would perform a night march and be ready at dawn to attack the main Magersfontein ridge. The cavalry would lead the initial approach, with the artillery and the Guards Brigade following behind with the intention of deploying to the right of the Highland Brigade prior to the dawn attack.

With six miles to go, the column set off in broad daylight at 2:00 p.m. on Sunday, December 10th, 1899. With Boer spies everywhere, it is unlikely this major movement would have been missed. Indeed, Methuen was painfully aware of the need for tight security and protection of his plans. Unfortunately, as a result, this meant he told only a few of the officers about the operation he had in mind. It was not until the Highland Brigade was opposite its objective later that evening that Wauchope and other senior officers were given the full battle plan. The soldiers themselves had no idea what they were doing.

The orders Wauchope received from Methuen might have been misunderstood by him. The Highland Brigade, faced with a taxing night march over unreconnoitred terrain, would have to move in a dense formation, with the soldiers holding knotted ropes to keep them close together in order not to lose their bearings or each other. Once in position for the assault, just before dawn, the brigade would shake out into battalions with five paces between soldiers. They would attack the eastern edge of Magersfontein Hill.

According to reports, Wauchope was not happy at the night march idea. The Highland Brigade bivouacked briefly in the open after dark to get some sleep. At 1:00 a.m. on the morning of December 11th, the close columns of soldiers moved off, guided by an artillery major named Benson.

Inevitably, things started to go wrong. A storm broke overhead, bringing disorientating thunder, lightning, and heavy rain. There was no moon, so it was pitch dark. The compasses were failing due to the iron content in the soil. Soldiers stumbled and cursed. Near dawn, the troops encountered some barbed wire entanglements, causing more delay, disruption, and confusion. The Boers had been on alert for some time.

At 4:00 a.m., Major Benson suggested to Wauchope that they were close enough to the Boer lines and should now spread out into extended lines. Wauchope hesitated. He was still concerned that his troops might wander off in different directions. He decided to continue in a dense grouping for a little while longer. It is possible that he had interpreted Methuen's orders to mean he should get very close before spreading out his troops. However, this was to be the undoing of Wauchope and his entire brigade.

A single shot cracked out, and at that noise, hundreds of Boers rifles began to fire rapidly. The Highland Brigade was just four hundred yards from the Boer trenches. The brigade was struck with confusion. No one issued any coherent orders, and contradictory shouts from officers and NCOs (non-commissioned officers) simply added to the chaos. Some groups spontaneously charged forward to attack the trenches, while others fell back. Others dropped to the ground and took cover.

The volume of rifle fire being directed into the compact mass of soldiers was ear-splitting and disorientating. It was not clear how many casualties were suffered by the Highlanders in those opening minutes. Since there was so much noise, Pemberton suggests that much of the Boer fire went overhead.[43] However, Sir Arthur Conan Doyle believed that the brigade suffered seven hundred casualties in the first five minutes.[44] But there was little scope for any decisive action on the part of the Highlanders. The Scottish battalions were pinned down for a large part of the day, and casualties steadily mounted.

The artillery tried to assist, firing on what Boer positions they thought they could identify. When daylight arrived, Methuen ordered the balloon to ascend to receive a real-time assessment of the situation. He brought up the 9th Brigade on the left of the railway to put pressure on the Boers.

After about nine hours of being shot at with scarce cover and minimal protection, the Highland Brigade understandably had had enough. The survivors withdrew from the battlefield, and the attack was over. At 5:30 in the early evening, the previously silent Boer artillery suddenly opened up on the British cavalry. More British troops started to withdraw. Methuen accepted the reality of the situation and ordered a general withdrawal back to the Modder River. General Wauchope's body was later recovered two hundred yards from the Boer trenches. The British had lost about one thousand soldiers (the Highland Brigade had lost seven hundred men, a quarter of its strength). The Boers lost around two hundred.

---

[43] Pemberton, W., *Battles of the Boer War*, (Pan Books, Ltd.: London, 1969), p.92.
[44] Doyle, C., "The Great Boer War," Chapter 9, Battle of Magersfontein, Sep. 1902, https://www.gutenberg.org/files/3069/3069-h/3069-h.htm

This ended Methuen's effective control over the offensive, and the drive on Kimberley stopped. Kimberley would have to wait until the new year, with a new military leadership, to be relieved.

The Battle of Stormberg

Stormberg was a small battle compared to Magersfontein and Colenso, but it was still highly damaging to the morale of the British public and the British forces in South Africa. Boer raiding forces pushed south into the Cape Colony and threatened pro-British townships, as well as some key railway lines from the south coast northward toward Bloemfontein in the Orange Free State.

General William Gatacre had a good reputation due to his solid performances as a brigadier and then a divisional commander under General Herbert Kitchener in the Sudan the previous year.[45] He was charged with protecting and, when necessary, repelling Boer raids in this area. Technically, he was the commander of the 3rd Division, but he did not have a full-strength force and had a smaller number of less experienced troops.

When Boer General Jan Olivier moved south to take the key rail junction of Stromberg, General Buller dithered, giving Gatacre vague instructions to try to retake the junction and repel the Boers. Gatacre's force was makeshift; initially, it was only one battalion strong, but further reinforcements from England, albeit inexperienced, brought Gatacre two more battalions and two artillery batteries. He felt he had enough soldiers to attempt to dislodge the Boers from a mountain position at Kissieberg, south of Stormberg.

He gathered a force of 2,600 men and 12 guns and began a night march to the Boer positions. The guide lost his way, and the British lost valuable time as a consequence. At dawn, the Boers spotted the British troops in the valley below and opened fire. The British soldiers attempted to scale the mountain slope, but it was too steep in most places. However, with the assistance of British artillery, the battle ebbed and flowed.

Other Boer forces arrived in the valley from the west, complicating the attack. Some of the British soldiers managed to ascend to the top,

---

[45] Kitchener was later a Field Marshal in the First World War. He died in 1916 when the battleship he was traveling in was sunk by a German mine.

and the Boers made preparations to withdraw. However, Gatacre, unsure of the situation, decided to withdraw. Unfortunately, some of the soldiers on the mountaintop did not receive the order. Due to this oversight, the next day, the Boers took six hundred British prisoners.

This battle effectively ended Gatacre's career, even though there was a lot of bad luck involved and many factors at play that were not entirely his fault, particularly the limited troop resources he had available as a divisional commander and Buller's poor instructions. The defeat did not particularly change the situation in this part of the Cape, and the Boers withdrew from Dordrecht. Gatacre resigned from the army in 1904 and died of fever in the Sudan in 1906.

The Battle of Colenso

Painting of Redvers Buller.
https://commons.wikimedia.org/wiki/File:VCRedversHenryBuller.jpg

The final battle of "Black Week" fell to Redvers Buller himself. He would suffer a painful defeat—ironically, almost all of it entirely self-inflicted—as he tried to move north over the Tugela River to relieve Ladysmith.

The Tugela was more challenging than the Modder River, as it was deeper, wider, and faster. The north bank of the Tugela River offered high ground, kops, and ridges, which were ideal for a defender resisting an attack from the south. But Colenso offered a clear and direct route to Ladysmith, with a rail bridge and railway to provide supplies for advancing British soldiers.

The Boer commander in this sector was Louis Botha, who was young, energetic, and skilled. He recognized that the north bank immediately beyond Colenso was flat. He favored allowing the British to cross over and then pin them down on the river line. Another key feature was the Hlangwane Hill, a steep feature to the east that was crucially on the south side of the river. This dominating hill was useful for both sides. Initially, the Boers garrisoned it, but it was isolated from the rest of the Boer defense line.

Botha had perhaps five thousand fighters, stretched from Bridle Drift in the west to Hlangwane Hill. Most were in concealed trenches. Buller had the largest single combined fighting force on either side in the whole of South Africa at the time. He had approximately sixteen thousand troops, including four infantry brigades, three cavalry regiments, and five batteries of artillery pieces, including two batteries of powerful naval 12-pounder guns. The artillery was commanded by Colonel Charles Long. His flawed decisions and the actions of his guns were to be a significant focal point of the battle.

Buller's initial plan was to buck the trend of the British battles thus far and conduct a flank attack at Potgieter's Drift, a crossing point some twenty-five miles west along the Tugela. He wanted to use some deception operations to allow the bulk of his force to sidestep the Boer defenses. An artillery barrage and a maneuvering brigade in the Colenso area would pin Botha's Boers and perhaps be aided by some form of military distraction from General White in Ladysmith while the rest of his force discreetly moved west.

Redvers Buller is a complex character. He was known for his bravery, which was proven by the Victoria Cross he earned twenty years previously during the Zulu War. He was also known to be concerned about the well-being of his troops. The soldiers loved him. However, he was prone to micromanage aspects of the logistics. He was indecisive, imprecise, and prone to overemotional moments.

Buller's carefully worked-out flanking plan took two hammer blows before it could be implemented: the news of the defeat at Stormberg and then Magersfontein. He became pessimistic about the whole outcome of the war and doubted whether he was the right man for the job.[46] In an instant, he overturned his carefully prepared plan, which had been scheduled for December 13th, fearing—as had Methuen— that it was too risky to abandon the safety of the railway supply line.

On December 14th, he summoned his brigade commanders together and told them they would attack Colenso at dawn the next day. This short-notice reversal came as a surprise to the officers. Buller's new plan was necessarily flawed:

"Adopted at so late an hour and after a brief re-examination by telescope of the Boer position, Buller's plan was necessarily vague and indefinite. No close reconnaissance of the Tugela had been made ... Like Methuen, Buller was without a proper map ... Nor, as specific orders did not reach the brigadiers till midnight, had they any opportunity of studying by daylight the ground allotted to them. All they knew was contained in the bleak opening words of those orders: 'The enemy is entrenched in the kopjes north of Colenso bridge.'"[47]

The plan envisaged three prongs of attack. Major General Arthur Fitzroy Hart's brigade would cross the Bridle Drift west of Colenso, Major General Henry Hildyard's brigade would cross at Colenso itself, and a small mounted infantry force under Lieutenant General Lord Douglas Dundonald would probe at Hlangwane. The orders were painfully imprecise, with confusion over where Hart was to cross the river and which of the two iron bridges at Colenso Hildyard was supposed to seize, given they pointed in very different directions. Dundonald was unsure what exactly he was supposed to do at Hlangwane.

Buller had not told General White in Ladysmith of the new plan, so there was no potential for a distraction from that direction.

The attack started at 4:30 a.m. The infantry brigades made their way in daylight over the several open miles that sloped gently down to the

---

[46] Pemberton, W., *Battles of the Boer War*, (Pan Books, Ltd.: London, 1969), pp.122-123.
[47] Pemberton, W., *Battles of the Boer War*, (Pan Books, Ltd.: London, 1969), pp.125.

river. The Boer positions were unknown. British artillery rounds landed on Fort Wylie just over the river. There was again over-confidence that the Boers were in small numbers or might have already fled at the impressive spectacle of thousands of British khaki-clad soldiers advancing in lines toward the Tugela. Again, there was discussion among the officers about having breakfast on the far side of the river.

Hart became hesitant over which direction his brigade should be taking. Buller's directions were unclear; he had only mentioned one small stream to cross where there were, in fact, two. It is also very possible that Buller was unaware of the true course of the river, which included a large loop. Hart's brigade moved off again, but it was moving into the loop, holding open the prospect of being shot at from three sides.

The Boers started shooting. Hart had no idea if there was a fordable drift at this point (there wasn't), and his troops, although under steady fire, could not identify anything to shoot back at.

Buller noticed this and suddenly became anxious. In the middle of the attack, he decided that Hart's attack should be called off and that Hart and his men should be pulled back.

At this point, Colonel Charles James Long, commander of the artillery batteries, enters the narrative. Long was aggressively proactive. From his discussions of the battle plan with Buller (with an entirely inadequate one-inch-to-the-mile Land Registry map), his interpretation was that he was to bring his heavy naval guns as far forward as possible, moving them from the relative safety of the rear to provide direct suppressive fire against the Boer positions on the north side.

The two batteries went forward. They outstripped Barton's brigade on the right and moved forward without any infantry support. Long's guns opened fire. They gave a good account of themselves, at one point firing one thousand shells in an hour. But they were exposed and highly vulnerable. They began to take casualties and had to pause as they ran out of ammunition. Many of the gun crews retired behind the guns while awaiting resupply.

Buller was once again concerned. From what he could see, the guns were too far forward and at great risk. He sent riders to see what state the guns and the gunners were in. Unfortunately, he received a garbled message in reply to the effect that the guns had been abandoned and most of the crew killed. This was incorrect. Nevertheless, Buller decided that not only should the guns be recovered and withdrawn at all costs but also that all his troops should retire.

This was the situation at 10:00 in the morning, with the battle barely underway. Hart's brigade was tangled up in a river dead end, suffering serious casualties. Hildyard had moved into Colenso, and the other two brigades—Lyttleton's and Barton's—had not been committed at all.

Buller immersed himself in the plight of Long's batteries, which were suffering casualties. Long himself was hit and died of his wounds close to his beloved guns. Buller appeared to have more or less lost control of the battle; he was no longer a general with a crucial strategic overview of developments. He was more like a junior officer, focused purely on one specific part of the battlefield at the exclusion of all else. When Buller moved forward to investigate the situation of Long's guns, an artillery shell landed close, killing his personal physician and injuring Buller. Pemberton suggests that, for the rest of the battle, Buller might have had shell shock.[48]

Buller spent time personally supervising the withdrawal of the brigades, which proved difficult since not all soldiers received the message. Some units were pinned under fire. Dundonald's small force of mounted infantry tried to take Hlangwane but came under heavy fire. He requested support from Barton's brigade, which was a few hundred yards away. Barton declined to help.

The efforts to save the guns continued. A small group of officer volunteers from Buller's staff raced toward the guns, determined to harness them to oxen and pull them to safety. One of them was Freddy Roberts, the only son of Field Marshal Lord Roberts. Freddy was a lieutenant with the King's Rifles. He had recently and spectacularly failed the entrance exam to Staff College. Field Marshal Lord Roberts had appealed to Field Marshal Wolseley, commander in chief of the British Army, for Freddy to be admitted to Staff College anyway. Wolseley rejected this request but said that an act of bravery on the battlefield might cause him to reconsider Freddy as a "special case." At Colenso, with the guns in peril, Freddy saw his chance to redeem his future and the respect of his father. The group of officers galloped forward and

---

[48] Pemberton, W., *Battles of the Boer War*, (Pan Books, Ltd.: London, 1969), p.137. Pemberton was writing in 1963. We might now use the term post-traumatic stress disorder or PTSD.

soon came under intense rifle fire from concealed Boer trenches. The officer accompanying Freddy was wounded three times. Freddy was shot off his horse and died shortly afterward on the battlefield.

The withdrawal began at 11:00 a.m. and was completed by around 2:00 p.m. Half the army had not been engaged at all. Buller's army painfully extracted itself and retired south to its camp. It had suffered well over a thousand soldiers killed, wounded, or captured and lost ten heavy guns and nine ammunition wagons as well.

Louis Botha agreed to the armistice requested by Buller. The next day was spent with ambulance teams and stretcher-bearers combing the battlefield and removing the dead and dying British soldiers. The Boers lost a minimal amount; one assessment gives a mere six killed and twenty-one wounded.

Once rested and recovered somewhat, Buller started blaming others for the misfortunes of the day, primarily Hart for getting into a dead end and Long for getting too far forward. Buller's mood was very low, and he had no appetite for returning to the fight with the two fresh brigades he still had the next morning.[49] In telegram dispatches written late that night, he suggested to White at Ladysmith that relief might not be possible and that White should perhaps consider surrendering. Buller wrote to London as well, stating that it was not possible to relieve White without a month-long siege of Colenso and that his army should now be on the defensive. In a final cable, he sent a message to Roberts about Freddy:

"Your gallant son died today. Condolences."

The analytical verdict on the conduct of the battle is mixed, although the concept and execution (the lack of reconnaissance, poor maps, short notice, vague orders, etc.) were clearly flawed. Pakenham feels that Buller made the correct decision to withdraw, given some of the early problems. Winston Churchill was also forgiving of Buller, thinking a lesser man would have pressed on with the attack and lost many more lives. However, one of the brigade commanders, Major General Neville Lyttleton, called it "one of the most unfortunate battles in which a British army has ever been engaged and in none has there been a more deplorable tactical display."[50]

---

[49] Some of his officers were very keen that the fight should be continued.
[50] Pemberton, W., *Battles of the Boer War*, (Pan Books, Ltd.: London, 1969), p.144.

The historian W. Baring Pemberton was also unimpressed.

"Colenso was a battle over before it had properly begun; a battle which has served ever since as an example of what ought not to be done in action."[51]

---

[51] Pemberton, W., *Battles of the Boer War*, (Pan Books, Ltd.: London, 1969), p.144.

Chapter 7 – The Second Phase: The Empire Strikes Back

Black Week was a painful shock to London, Britain, and the British Empire. Indeed, the whole of November and December had been a series of embarrassments for the British. For much of the British press and many of the politicians, a rabble of Bible-bashing ignorant farmers armed with highly modern weapons had humiliated the greatest empire in the world.[52] But after the initial impact, the mood quickly became that of grim determination and resolve.[53] Depression was replaced with recognition that this was not to be a short war but a hard slog that would need many more resources than were currently available.

Some shake-ups in the command structure were needed. The famous Field Marshal Lord Roberts, then commander of the British forces in Ireland, was brought back to London and given the appointment of the

---

[52] Des Latham, the South African Boer War historian, sees a lot of similarities with the Taliban's performance against the US and international forces in Afghanistan from 2001 to 2021.

[53] It is worth noting that a minor bit of excitement in the British press at this time was caused by the news that Winston Churchill, after a month in captivity at the hands of the Boers, had managed to escape on December 12th. He was commended by Buller and given a temporary post as an officer in a cavalry unit, from where he continued to observe the campaign. Entering Pretoria with British forces in June 1900, he liberated the prison of its remaining British soldiers. When he eventually returned to Britain, he was something of a hero and well placed for a move into politics. Klein, C., 'The Daring Escape That Forged Winston Churchill,' *History*, 28 Mar. 2023, https://www.history.com/news/the-daring-escape-that-forged-winston-churchill

commander of British forces in South Africa. Although he replaced Buller, Buller was not actually sacked.[54] Instead, Buller became General Officer Commanding (GOC) British forces in Natal. He would have one more opportunity to push British forces into a battlefield disaster.

Britain slowly began to understand that it needed to scale up its approach to war. As Packenham notes, Britain had been used to fighting a war "on the cheap" against tribes.[55] A more industrial-scale approach was needed. Volunteers and reinforcements from the UK and the British Empire began to arrive. The trickle became a stream. There was a strong sense of the empire becoming united in this adversity. Major government funds were being pushed toward the War Office. Where financiers had previously balked at expenditures of £500,000, now preparations were being made for a new £10 million investment in all things military.[56]

Canadians and Australians arrived in South Africa. Imperial Yeomanry volunteers, raised from local counties and communities, came from Britain. There was suddenly a shortage of khaki dye and cloth to make uniforms.

In January 1900, the 5th Division, under General Sir Charles Warren, arrived in South Africa, and more divisions were planned to arrive. This was now the largest British force ever to have been sent overseas. The division was sent off to join Buller's force in Natal.

Field Marshal Roberts arrived in Cape Town on January 11th and was now in charge. He brought with him a key figure as his chief of staff: Lieutenant General Lord Herbert Kitchener. Already famous for his campaign in the Sudan the previous year (including the defeat of the Dervish army at Omdurman), Kitchener brought considerable organizational skills and energy. He would also become notorious for the concentration camps that were later set up to detain the Boer population.

Roberts's initial assessments of the state of the three besieged towns were almost as bleak as Buller's had been. He suggested that perhaps, after all, it might be better to abandon them. After further analysis and

---

[54] Even though many officers and politicians felt that he should have been.
[55] Pakenham, T., *The Boer War*, (Abacus: London 2022), p. 247.
[56] The final total cost of the war to Britain has since been calculated at over £200 million.

consultation, however, he decided that the Buller strategy should remain broadly unchanged and that the two reinforced British forces should continue their attacks on Ladysmith and Kimberley.

President Kruger and the Boers were now faced with a bigger set of challenges to which the answers appeared increasingly limited. Launching raids and inflicting casualties in the hope the British would concede seemed to be the only realistic option. After a successful British raid against Boer hilltop gun positions overlooking Ladysmith on December 8th, 1899, the Boer leadership approved a large-scale surprise attack against Ladysmith on January 6th. Although it certainly caused casualties to the British, the Boers also suffered heavily, and it was judged unsuccessful.

The Bloodiest Battle: Spion Kop

To continue the southern push to relieve Ladysmith, Roberts left Buller in charge. General Warren and the 5th Division joined Buller, bringing an extra two infantry brigades, over two thousand cavalry, and thirty-six more artillery pieces. However, Warren had been brought out of retirement and had little recent combat experience. Buller was unhappy at having been marginalized and resented Warren's arrival.

The new plan of attack to get over the Tugela River was Buller's original concept of a flank attack upstream at Potgieter's Drift. The plan now was for two prongs to cross the Tugela, one at Potgieter's and the other at Trikhardt's Drift, a further six miles upstream. On January 16th, 1900, Dundonald's mounted troops managed to cross at the Potgieter ferry; British troops were now on the north bank of the Tugela.

This was good news, but Buller and Warren were both naturally cautious. Buller wanted Warren to take the Trikhardt crossing before he moved forward from Potgieter. Buller gave two-thirds of the force to Warren for this task for reasons that are unclear. Buller was placing most of the responsibility for a successful attack on Warren, who, with his slow movement of supplies and insistence on rehearsals and preparation, was already starting to vex Buller, who was demanding rapid movement.

Boers at Spion Kop.
https://commons.wikimedia.org/wiki/File:Boers_at_Spion_Kop,_1900_-_Project_Gutenberg_eText_16462.jpg

 The Boers watched the slow maneuvers of Warren's troops from the hilltops. Using African forced labor to dig trenches, they were able to keep pace with the British.

 The Tugela was a difficult river, and the terrain, with its steep, tall, rocky mountains, was forbidding. Winston Churchill, who was literally back in the saddle and still writing for *The Morning Post* while notionally attached to a cavalry unit, conducted his own reconnaissance. He was concerned by the sheer six-hundred-foot cliffs that dominated much of the river's course.[57] He would later describe the flat top of Spion Kop as "about as large as Trafalgar Square. Into this confined area 2,000 British infantry were packed."[58]

 On the night of January 23rd, Warren's 10th Brigade, under Lieutenant Colonel Thorneycroft, was sent to scale the heights of Spion Kop, which both sides recognized was the key place to be controlled along this stretch of the Tugela. The soldiers reached the top and encountered a

---

[57] Latham, D., The Anglo-Boer War podcast, episode eighteen, https://www.abwarpodcast.com/
[58] Churchill, W., My Early Life, A Roving Commission (R. Maclehose and Co.: London 1944), p. 324.

handful of sentries who ran away after a brief firefight. The British had successfully taken Spion Kop more or less without a shot being fired.

Some engineers set to work digging trenches. They had only brought twenty pickaxes and twenty shovels for a thousand men. The other soldiers sat back in relief and relaxed. The engineers discovered, after a foot or two of digging, that they struck rock, leaving the trenches shallow and inadequate. It was misty. A message of success was instantly sent back to Warren, Buller, Roberts, and even London (such was the power of the telegraph by that point), saying that Spion Kop was in British hands.

When dawn broke and the mist had cleared, Thorneycroft's men discovered a serious problem. They had dug in in the wrong place. The mountain had a flat top, and they were overlooked by three or four Boer hilltop positions manned by artillery and riflemen. Hidden "dead" ground and gently sloping crests made it hard to identify where the Boers were.

The Boers scrambled to reorientate their artillery. They launched a quick infantry counterattack and pinned the British down. The British began to realize the inadequacies of last night's entrenching efforts. Boer artillery shells landed regularly, sometimes ten in a minute, on the flat unprotected hilltop defended by the 10th Brigade. Casualties mounted rapidly. Subsequently, it was discovered that many soldiers were hit on the right side of their head because Boer sharpshooters had moved unseen up the east side of the hill. Other hill peaks to the east—Twin Peaks, Aloe Knoll, and Conical Hill—offered dominating views of the ground for the Boers. Spion Kop was swept by gunfire from several different directions. General Woodgate, the senior British commander on Spion Kop, was hit in the head by a bursting artillery round and was seriously wounded and evacuated.

Back at headquarters, General Warren had no real idea what was going on until he received a terse note flashed by heliograph: "Send reinforcements at once or all is lost. General dead."[59]

Warren's response was sluggish and confused. The mist was still clinging to his side of the mountain. It was difficult to locate the sound of firing. Previous reports from Spion Kop had been positive. He was still

---

[59] Pemberton, W., *Battles of the Boer War*, (Pan Books, Ltd.: London, 1969), p.172.

worried about his forces on the left flank by the Tabanyama ridge to the northwest of Spion Kop.

With Woodgate out of action, officers replaced him, but they were all killed. Only Lieutenant Colonel Thorneycroft remained. The hail of fire continued. Buller fussed and unhelpfully micromanaged Warren from a distance, even though he had an even less clear understanding of the situation than Warren. Buller insisted that Thorneycroft be placed in charge of the troops on Spion Kop. A message was eventually sent telling Thorneycroft that he was now the general in charge of the defenders.

A couple of British battalions, the Middlesex Regiment and the Imperial Light Infantry, were sent up the hill to reinforce Thorneycroft. They were immediately flung into a counterattack to prevent the Boers from overrunning the British positions. A Scottish battalion also made its way up. Some British troops started to wave white handkerchiefs in a bid to surrender. The Boers moved forward to take their surrender. It was only Thorneycroft's personal intervention—largely by shouting—that stopped this. The Boers withdrew, and the fighting continued.

Communications between the top and Warren's headquarters were minimal. In the absence of any significant direction or leadership from Warren and Buller, Winston Churchill, incredibly, twice ascended to the top to communicate with the beleaguered Thorneycroft, assess the situation, and report back to Warren.

By a curious twist of fate, during the course of Churchill's ascents and descents, it seems highly likely that he came in close proximity to the great Indian leader Mahatma Gandhi, who was part of the Natal Indian Ambulance Corps.

Thorneycroft was traumatized by the losses and the lack of any plan conveyed to him. He and his men had been under fire for sixteen hours without food, water, or, crucially, instructions. He had already decided to withdraw from the hill that night, and he brought his battered survivors off the hill without understanding how close he had been to receiving reinforcements and how near the Boers themselves had been to withdrawing from the hill. The British had lost 250 killed and 1,250 wounded or captured. The Boers had lost 335 killed and wounded.

Spion Kop was another catastrophic failure for the British military system. But in early February, with Roberts in charge, momentum, better organization, and more supplies and soldiers ensured that the tempo of operations began to pick up.

More divisions arrived from Britain. General Kelly-Kenny's 6th Division arrived in late January, with the 7th, 8th, and 9th Divisions also scheduled to arrive. However, gathering such a large force required compromises. Many of the soldiers and mounted troopers were irregular, locally recruited men or Uitlanders. Their training was not good, their military effectiveness was poor, and they were not averse to looting and engaging in other human rights abuses.

Buller resumed his attempts to get over the Tugela. From February 5th to 7th, he fought and failed to get a crossing east of Spion Kop. The Battle of Vaal Krantz was inconclusive, costing Buller's force 350 casualties and the Boers thirty dead and fifty wounded.

Buller's fourth attempt, on February 12th, was northeast of Colenso. Buller was slowly learning to use his mobile forces more effectively, and the infantry units were developing a better understanding of the need to make use of the terrain for protection and cover, moving forward in small groups in short rushes rather than densely packed lines and columns. The British were slowly adopting Boer techniques.

Dundonald's cavalry brigade and Lyttleton's 4th Division managed to secure the high ground, which meant the Boers had to abandon Hlangwane Hill and pull back. The Boers were slowly retreating, and Buller's force pushed forward, continually looking for ways to outflank the diminishing number of Boer forces. At the Battle of Pieters Hill on February 27th, amid bitter resistance from the Boers, the British broke through the Boer defenses, and the Boers retreated.

Boer resistance in front of Ladysmith was effectively over. On February 28th, General Buller rode at the head of his troops to meet General White inside Ladysmith. The siege had ended.

Meanwhile, back at the Modder River, Roberts and his chief of staff, Kitchener, were making their own plans for a new offensive to come to the aid of Kimberley. The Boers, having effectively resisted Methuen's attacks in December, still held the Magersfontein high ground. It remained a formidable position and dominated the direct route to Kimberley. This time, however, the team of Roberts, Kitchener, and General French, now commanding an entire horse-borne division of some five thousand cavalry and mounted infantry, were actively planning to outflank the imposing ridge and make a dash for Kimberley.

The coordinated operation worked well. A small infantry force maneuvered to the west of Magersfontein, distracting Cronje and causing him to move some of his Boers over to that side just to be safe. Then, French's cavalry division moved southeast to cross the Riet River at Klipdrift before driving northeast to bypass Magersfontein. Once past the Boer positions, he turned northwest and moved at high speed for Kimberley.

This time, the Boers had no answer for such a large and mobile force, either at Magersfontein or Kimberley. The Boers' besieging artillery pieces fired a few parting salvoes into the town before the gun crews and soldiers packed up and moved off.

On February 15th, General French entered Kimberley to the great excitement of the population. That evening, he and his officers were invited to a champagne reception at Cecil Rhodes's house. But French had no time for this. He needed to tend to his troops and issue orders for the continued pursuit of General Cronje's forces.

French had a significant problem to deal with. Although he had not suffered many casualties among his troops, his "cavalry charge" to relieve Kimberley had come at a high price for the horses. His route along the veld was scattered with the corpses of horses. They had not been acclimatized to the terrain, had been ridden hard, and were not always able to drink water. Many had collapsed and died. For a division of five thousand, French now had less than one and a half thousand mounts.

Early next morning, French's reduced force headed southeast, looking for the retreating Boers who had left the Magersfontein entrenchments. He would find them twenty-five miles southeast of Kimberley at Paardeberg Drift.

French stumbled upon these Boers as they were resting and regrouping on the banks of the Modder River. The Boer artillery chased the British cavalry away, but Cronje's force of about five thousand men had been located, and there was a high likelihood that more substantial British forces would soon be on the way. Cronje had to make a quick decision: fight or flight.

Paardeberg ("Horse Mountain") was not a good location to stand up to the British, but Cronje dithered before deciding to stay. This was probably a bad call. In the face of overwhelming numbers bearing down on him, he probably should have taken advantage of the high mobility of the Boer forces. However, many Boer wives, children, and other noncombatants, along with slow-moving ox carts, were in the encampment. If the soldiers escaped, it would mean leaving Boer families to an uncertain fate.

Cronje elected to stand and fight, forming a laager and digging trenches on the riverbank. It was to be a decisive mistake and, after a battle lasting over a week, would lead to the surrender of the Boer army in this area.

This time, the British had superior forces and artillery. General Kelly-Kenny's 6th Division was brought up, and the Boers were surrounded. Kelly-Kenny's plan was sensible; he wanted to keep the Boers penned in and hungry while bombarding them until they surrendered. In his view, there was no need to launch a potentially costly infantry attack.

However, Roberts became temporarily ill with the flu. Kitchener was in charge in Roberts's absence and demanded a quicker result with some frontal assaults, which would have inevitable consequences. On February 18th, battalions from Kelly-Kenny's division were pushed into battle and suffered disproportionate casualties—well over a thousand—for no gain. However, the Boers had suffered as well, particularly from the British artillery bombardments. They had lost many wagons, supplies, and horses, reducing their mobility and ability to sustain combat operations.[60]

Field Marshal Roberts resumed command of the battle on February 19th. He was considering whether to withdraw his forces to recover from the losses they had sustained. On February 21st, the Boers withdrew from one of the hills of their defense line. It looked as if the Boers' will to resist was weakening. Roberts decided to stay. On February 26th, Canadian soldiers moved their positions forward and dug trenches within one hundred yards of the Boer front lines. On February 27th, General Cronje decided that his forces could not continue the fight. He and four thousand soldiers surrendered to Roberts.[61]

Cronje and the four thousand captured at Paardeberg were sent to a prison on the island of Saint Helena, where they would cause no further trouble.[62] So, the Boers were now under real pressure. Ladysmith and Kimberley had been relieved. The Boers had lost several military engagements, including the first major surrender of Boer commandos.

---

[60] 'Battle of Paardeberg, *Great Boer War*, https://www.britishbattles.com/great-boer-war/battle-of-paardeberg/

[61] Pakenham, T., *The Boer War*, (Abacus: London 2022), p. 342.

[62] Incidentally, this was where Napoleon Bonaparte was finally sent into exile after his defeat at the Battle of Waterloo.

The situation began to look bleak, as the slowly moving British picked up speed and momentum.

The lifting of the sieges had caused great enthusiasm back in Britain. Now, it seemed as if the Boer capitals—the Orange Free State's Bloemfontein and the Transvaal's Pretoria—were at real risk. It also seemed that the British were starting to absorb the military lessons from the campaign, such as the importance of mobility, coordination, concealed movement, good intelligence, and reconnaissance. The British troops were making use of spacing, cover, and concealment.

Roberts began the advance on Bloemfontein. The Boers on both the southern and western fronts appeared demoralized and less willing to put up a resistance. Christiaan de Wet, a committed and skilled commander, took over control of the Boer troops in the area after Cronje's surrender. De Wet quickly gathered together what fighters he could (some six thousand or so) and threw up a screen ten miles wide on both sides of the Modder River centered on Poplar Grove in an effort to protect Bloemfontein, which was some fifty miles to the east. On March 7th, President Kruger visited the Boer fighters at Poplar Grove. But he had to leave very quickly when reports came in that Roberts and the British were approaching.

Roberts's plan of attack at Poplar Grove was based on the lessons of French's outflanking of Magersfontein and the fact that de Wet's men had constructed extensive defensive positions. French would again push northeast and loop around the Boer positions to cut off their retreat. However, his assumptions were flawed. The Boers, once it was clear what was going on, started to retreat of their own free will, despite de Wet's attempts to restore order and conduct a rearguard action.

Roberts was frustrated; the prize of encircling and capturing Kruger, de Wet, and six thousand fighters was not to be his. French's cavalry were slow. Many horses were exhausted and poorly treated. De Wet conducted an effective mobile defense, given that many of his soldiers no longer wanted to stay and fight.

After the Boers' retreat from Poplar Grove, they fell back twenty miles to Abraham's Kraal before they dispersed again, with many opting to return home. Field Marshal Roberts's soldiers entered Bloemfontein on March 13th. There was no military opposition. The capture of Bloemfontein went peacefully. Roberts was keen to avoid provocation and allow the Boers to come to terms with British rule. He allowed most of the Boer city officials to remain in their posts to continue the necessary administration.[63]

This allowed Roberts to turn his attention to Mafeking, where a force of two thousand British, under the spirited leadership of Colonel Baden-Powell, had been resisting two thousand Boer besiegers for nearly seven months. Once it became clear to the Boers that a British relief force was on the way, the Boers made an attempt to storm the town before the British arrived. On May 12th, 240 Boers, under the command of a young officer called Sarel Eloff, launched a daring nighttime raid, capturing the police barracks. After the initial surprise had worn off, the British surrounded the Boer force.

Although Eloff's men held out for the next day, they surrendered later the next evening. On May 17th, 1900, a British flying column of two thousand under Colonel Mahon brushed past limited Boer opposition and relieved Mafeking to ecstatic scenes of rejoicing across the town and much of the English-speaking world. The relief of Mafeking became a culturally symbolic moment in British history, a cliché even. Many towns in Britain acquired a "Mafeking Street" in the years to follow. "To Maffick" became a verb meaning to party with excitement.[64]

Perhaps more significant than the relief of Mafeking was Roberts's announcement on May 28th that the Orange Free State's existence was now at an end and was to become a British colony again, named the Orange River Colony.

Everything had moved very quickly and successfully for the British in the last few weeks. Now, the Transvaal was well and truly in Roberts's sights. However, it was suddenly hard to move forward, as a series of non-military difficulties struck the British. They needed time to regroup and reorganize since the logistics and medical systems had been stretched to the point of collapse. Partly as a result of poor food and water supplies, soldiers had been drinking from unhealthy water sources. Outbreaks of typhoid had struck the British troops hard. Many died or were hospitalized.

Much of the military effort simply revolved around moving thousands of new British troops in dusty columns forward, farther into the Boer

---

[63] Pakenham, T., *The Boer War*, (Abacus: London 2022), p. 375.
[64] Pakenham, T., *The Boer War*, (Abacus: London 2022), pp.416-417.

provinces. Some of the mounted units performed the impressive feat of moving 260 miles in 26 days.[65] Resistance from the Boers was dwindling.

"The pattern of advance rarely faltered. The enemy was the veld, not the Boers: a sun to fry you and a frost to freeze you (for winter had come, encrusting the men's blankets with hoar frost as they slept), too little trek ox to eat, to few biscuits—when there were rations at all."[66]

Although there were some actions as British columns encountered Boer rearguards, the Boers generally retreated faster than the British could advance. At each of the rivers that could have afforded a viable defensive line, the Boers dug trenches as if preparing for a defense. When the British arrived, the Boers simply packed up and retreated farther back. A Boer unit of Irishmen, self-styled the "Wrecker Corps," perfected the art of blowing up bridges and railway sidings, leaving plumes of black smoke smearing the horizon as the British pushed forward.

On May 28th, a symbolic and bloody clash took place at Doornkop. Doornkop was the infamous location of Dr. Jameson's last stand in 1895. The Boers had drawn up forces to resist a much more powerful British force. The Boers chose a good defensive line on a ridge that was actually two ridges with some dead ground in between. Colonel Ian Hamilton, who had recently been liberated from the siege of Ladysmith, had been promoted to general and now had command of two brigades of soldiers. The British advance had been halted by some Boer artillery fire.

Doornkop was to be one of the last large-scale actions of the Boer War. It brought an interesting and bloody contrast between British tactics and learning processes. Two infantry battalions took part in the attack. One battalion, the Gordon Highlanders, was a regular army unit that had also fought at Majuba in 1881. The other, the City Imperial Volunteers (CIV) from London, were newly formed for the campaign and had none of the "old school" concepts of attacking line by line.

The Highlanders marched forward in lines and suffered high casualties, losing one hundred men in ten minutes. The CIV, however, performed well in the attack at a much lower cost in lives. The CIV

---

[65] Pakenham, T., *The Boer War*, (Abacus: London 2022), p.419.
[66] Pakenham, T., *The Boer War*, (Abacus: London 2022), p.419.

infantry advanced in small groups, rushing forward while other groups provided covering fire. This is a fundamental principle of modern warfare. Because of the casualties suffered, questions were asked about Hamilton's decision to conduct a frontal attack and even if an attack was necessary, given there were opportunities to move around the Boer right flank. Hamilton had been locked up under siege in Ladysmith and had probably not absorbed some of the lessons of the new modern warfare being fought out in South Africa. Perhaps he also wanted some revenge for his experiences at the Boers' hands.[67]

With British forces now pressing on Johannesburg from the west and east, nothing was going to save the Boers. On May 31st, Johannesburg was captured, and Pretoria fell a week later, on June 5th. President Paul Kruger and his supporters left Pretoria on May 29th. Kruger left his wife behind, and he would never see her again. She was unwell and would die the next year while Kruger was in exile in Europe.

The Boers—civilians, soldiers, and political leaders—were deeply divided about what to do next. Many wanted to continue the fight. They became known as the "Bitter Enders." But many others, having also fought bravely, now felt that the fight was over and that it was time to return to their families and pick up the pieces.

Roberts was keen to avoid humiliating the Boers. Some fighters had surrendered, and others had accepted the amnesty offered by Roberts the previous March. The "Bitter Enders" saw this as a betrayal and called them the "Hands-uppers."[68] The Boer commander Christiaan de Wet threatened to shoot his brother, Piet de Wet, when he learned that Piet wanted to surrender. Kruger consulted with President Steyn of the Orange Free State. Steyn wanted to continue the fight, which heartened Kruger.

It should have been a warning to Roberts and the British government that the Boers did not surrender when both their capitals had fallen to the British. There were still many armed and mounted Boer groups (and many talented and committed military commanders) in and around the Transvaal and the former Orange Free State. As a result, there were some more small-scale battles to be fought in this stage of the conflict.

---

[67] Pakenham, T., *The Boer War*, (Abacus: London 2022), p.426.
[68] Pakenham, T., *The Boer War*, (Abacus: London 2022), p.488.

Between June 11th and 12th, two Boer generals, Louis Botha and Koos de la Rey, along with six thousand fighters and thirty guns, confronted fourteen thousand British soldiers east of Pretoria at Diamond Hill. After fierce fighting, the Boers withdrew, but they had been encouraged by their performance against the British. In late August, a series of actions were fought between August 21st and 27th at Bergendal. Again, the Boers were forced to withdraw, but their main force remained intact. The Boers dispersed, only to regroup again later.

On September 3rd, 1900, Roberts declared the war over. Thousands of Boer prisoners were sent abroad to Saint Helena, Ceylon, Bermuda, and India. The South African Republic (the Transvaal) was formerly annexed by Britain. Paul Kruger fled the Transvaal, first to Portuguese East Africa (now Mozambique) and then via ship to the Netherlands. He was sympathetically received but played no further significant part in the story. Steyn briefly joined Kruger but returned later to South Africa. Kruger died in Switzerland in July 1904. The British allowed his body to be returned to Pretoria for a state funeral in December 1904.

Chapter 8 – The Third Phase: Guerrilla Warfare

To the British, it was simple. They had captured the enemy capitals, and the Boer leadership had fled into exile. Therefore, the war was over, with the British as the outright victors.

However, the Boer War did not end yet—only one phase of it had. A new and more brutal period was beginning. The Boers could no longer field a conventional army to compete with the hundreds of thousands of British soldiers now in South Africa. But they could return to their key strengths: their ability to move in small, fast groups, live off the land, and strike the British anywhere they found them. And the extensive British supply lines, depots, railways, and other lines of communication would provide excellent targets. As the British soon found out, they often only controlled the area that they physically occupied. Every other place belonged to the Boers. Like guerrilla groups throughout history, perhaps the Boer commandos thought they could simply wear down and exhaust the British and cause them to withdraw.

By the autumn, the British were complacent and congratulating themselves. On September 26th, in Britain, a general election was held. The governing Conservative Party believed they could capitalize on having just won a war (or so they thought). The so-called "khaki election" returned the Conservatives to power.

In South Africa, General Buller returned to England in October. In November, Field Marshal Roberts handed over control of the army to

Lord Kitchener and returned to England in December. British troop numbers were scaled down, and less experienced forces were left behind. But Milner was worried about a guerrilla war. He felt that Roberts and Kitchener did not understand the risks. He wrote to the newly appointed minister of war, St John Brodrick, to express his concerns.

"The letter, written in early November, predicted disaster in South Africa unless they adopted a more systematic military strategy ... the war was not, as Roberts claimed 'practically over.' It had burst out in October in a more virulent form: guerrilla war. Milner put the blame fairly and squarely on Roberts."[69]

The Boers had already been employing guerrilla tactics quite successfully for some while. On March 31st, 1900, 2,000 fighters under Christiaan and Piet de Wet launched an ambush at Sanna Post that killed 150 British and captured over 400 soldiers and 7 guns.

At Lindley, on May 29th, 1900, a British battalion of Imperial Yeomanry under Colonel Basil Spragge was surrounded by fighters under Piet de Wet. On May 31st, the battalion surrendered, and the Boers took over four hundred prisoners.[70] In early June, the Boer army amounted to only eight thousand fighters, as many had surrendered or taken the amnesty. Christiaan de Wet, with only eight hundred soldiers now, targeted the British communications routes.

"The next day, de Wet ambushed a convoy carrying supplies from the railway to General Colville and the Highland Brigade at Heilbron; the telegraph wires had first been cut, so the officer in charge did not receive Colville's warning against sending the convoy without a decent escort. The convoy was duly snapped up by de Wet, without firing a shot; this supplied him with 56 food wagons and 160 prisoners, mainly Highlanders."[71]

The two Boer governments reached an agreement for the use of guerrilla war tactics. They were concerned about the impact this might have on the civilian populace, particularly the women and children left

---

[69] Pakenham, T., *The Boer War*, (Abacus: London 2022), p.468.

[70] Gordon, A., "Battle of Lindley – 31 May 1900," *Battle Tours ZA*, 31 May 2020, https://www.battletoursza.com/battle-of-lindley-31-may-1900/

[71] Pakenham, T., *The Boer War*, (Abacus: London 2022), p.435.

behind in isolated farmsteads: Roberts had already demonstrated a willingness to burn farms.

The Boer commandos had better opportunities to ambush British supply lines. Koos de la Rey proved to be another tenacious commander with the skills and temperament for guerrilla fighting. On December 2nd, his commandos ambushed an ox-drawn supply convoy. He took fifty-four prisoners and seized over one hundred wagons of supplies. Unable to absorb this large quantity of prisoners and booty, the commandos took what they could, released the prisoners, and burned the supply column.

In mid-December, Koos de la Rey was reinforced by another commando. They launched an attack on a British base at Nooitgedacht. The British lost over six hundred killed, wounded, or captured. The stocks of supplies in the camp were comprehensively looted by the Boers.

The Boer commandos depended upon local support and their ability to move faster than the British. They lived off the land and what they could loot from British supply columns. They generally stayed in the local areas that they were familiar with, benefiting from an intimate understanding of the territory they were operating in.[72]

Kitchener began to find the new Boer approach a protracted strain.[73] However, it was not always easy for the Boers. They struggled with a fragmented commander structure. Boer generals operated on their own for a long time and were out of contact with the leadership. One of the best Boer commanders was Christiaan de Wet, but even he had several narrow escapes from the British. The Boers' strategy was lacking; they did not really know what they were trying to do or how to do it. They argued with other commanders, fearing that some were willing to give up or enter into talks with the British.

The British response began to get more coordinated as 1901 began. A key priority was to protect the railway lines and supply routes. The concept of "blockhouses" was introduced in South Africa. The idea of small, simple forts built at regular intervals to protect a railway line or divide up an area to be cleared originated from the Spanish-American

---

[72] Childs, S., 'Some Lessons and Effects of the Anglo-Boer War (1899-1902),' June 2022.
[73] Pakenham, T., *The Boer War*, (Abacus: London 2022), pp.534-535.

War in Cuba in 1898. Roberts had initiated the principle in South Africa, but it was Kitchener, in 1901, who perfected and expanded the construction.

The forts were reinforced by stone walls and screened by barbed wire. They were placed at regular intervals along a route within visual range of the forts on either side. They were manned by half a dozen soldiers and were two or three stories high in order to afford a good view of the surrounding area. The barbed wire greatly reduced the Boers' mobility.[74]

Around eight thousand blockhouses were built by the end of the war. Although they took three months to build and early prototypes cost £1,000 each, the cost and time were reduced as mass production got under way.[75] Fifty thousand soldiers lived in these blockhouses, which stretched over six thousand kilometers. The blockhouse system was crude but effective.[76]

The British had other unpleasant tricks up their sleeve. Aggressive flying columns hounded the Boer commandos. Many of these units included armed Africans, whom the Boers feared might take particular revenge on Boer families. The columns adopted a scorched-earth policy, which means they burned, destroyed, or looted anything of value, including farms, houses, food supplies, and crops. Zulu tribes were encouraged to loot Boer cattle herds. An extension of the scorched-earth approach included the relocation of thousands of Boer families—women, children, and native African workers—and "concentrating" them in tented camps away from their homes and from the Boer guerrillas.

Concentration Camps

"In early March, Kitchener decided to break the [guerrilla] stalemate by a double sweeping operation: to flush out the guerrillas ... and to sweep the country bare of everything that could give sustenance to the guerrillas ... But where could the women and children be put, if removed from their homes? ... it was the clearance of civilians —uprooting a whole

---

[74] 'Blockhouses of the Boer War,' *The Australian Boer War Memorial*, website accessed 11 Dec. 2023, https://www.bwm.org.au/blockhouses.php

[75] Thomas Pakenham thinks they only cost £16 by the end, Pakenham, T., *The Boer War*, (Abacus: London 2022), p.526.

[76] Pakenham, T., *The Boer War*, (Abacus: London 2022), p.537.

nation—that would come to dominate the last phase of the war."[77]

The policy of concentrating thousands of civilians in camps was approved by Kitchener as a quick solution to end the war. The plan was simple, the resources limited, and the outcome horrific. Tented accommodations were to house thousands of women and children in close proximity. Rations were limited and of poor quality. The tents were generally inadequate for the heat of the day or the freezing cold of the night. Crucially, medical resources and facilities for sanitation and hygiene were limited. The young, elderly, and infirm were highly vulnerable, and disease spread rapidly. People began to die. Even the government in London was getting anxious about some of the reports it was hearing from the camps. Historians seem to agree that Kitchener did not intend this to be the result. However, he did not seem to care much either and seemed happy to minimize or ignore what was rapidly becoming a major humanitarian disaster.[78]

Around forty to fifty thousand people died in the concentration camps; approximately half were Boer women and children, and half were black Africans who had been similarly detained.[79]

Many tried to alleviate the suffering of the vulnerable people in the camps or draw attention to their plight. Emily Hobhouse's work is worth attention. A British humanitarian campaigner and political activist, she was opposed to the war in South Africa. When she heard about the British military plans to "concentrate" Boer populations, she visited South Africa to assess the camps herself. She wanted to understand what the British authorities were doing and to try and alleviate the plight of the civilians where possible.[80]

Her reports helped to focus attention and ring alarm bells. On one visit to South Africa, she was arrested and sent back to Britain. There was growing unease in Britain. Members of Parliament were becoming

---

[77] Pakenham, T., *The Boer War*, (Abacus: London 2022), p.493.
[78] Pakenham, T., *The Boer War*, (Abacus: London 2022), p.493.
[79] "Concentration Camps in the South African War? Here Are the Real Facts," *University of Pretoria*, website accessed, 5 Mar. 2023, https://www.up.ac.za/research-matters/news/post_2999519-concentration-camps-in-the-south-african-war-here-are-the-real-facts.
[80] "Emily Hobhouse," *South African History online*, website accessed, 11 Dec. 2023, https://www.sahistory.org.za/people/emily-hobhouse

concerned. Hobhouse's work was instrumental in bringing the issue into the public domain.

Concentration camp improvements were minimal and ineffectual; there were never enough resources or finances to make the necessary improvements, even when the military officials were willing. Kitchener's sweeps continued to bring more and more civilians into the camps, and the death toll began to climb.[81]

---

[81] Pakenham, T., *The Boer War*, (Abacus: London 2022), pp.507-508.

Chapter 9 – Defeat

Boer resistance remained fierce at the end of 1901 and the beginning of 1902. However, it was becoming more erratic, and the Boers were not always successful. Even the best Boer commanders were having very narrow escapes and suffering defeats. But the actions continued. On October 30th, 1901, Louis Botha attacked the rearguard of a British flying column, killing seventy-three British at a loss of fourteen of his own men.

On December 25th, 1901, Christiaan de Wet's commandos were operating in the northeast of the Transvaal. They stealthily occupied a hilltop overlooking a camp of British soldiers protecting the construction of a line of blockhouses. The surprise attack resulted in 150 British dead and wounded, and the Boers gathered up over 200 prisoners. The Boers suffered forty dead and wounded.

Koos de la Rey, in the western Transvaal, was also active. He conducted significant ambushes against the British on February 25th and again on March 7th, 1902. This latter action at Tweebosch was a particular embarrassment for the British, who had over a thousand mounted soldiers and four guns. The troops were largely inexperienced, but they were under the direct command of General Methuen of Magersfontein fame. Many British troops fled the battlefield. Methuen was wounded twice and broke a leg when his horse fell on him. To add insult to injury, he was then taken prisoner by the Boers.[82] It was a

---

[82] Methuen was later released by the Boer commander Koos de la Rey because his injuries were

disaster and a humiliation. It was also a shock to Kitchener:

"The news of Methuen's smash-up at Tweebosch was telegraphed to Kitchener next day, and the news knocked him. A column of twelve hundred men, with four field guns, virtually wiped out: it was the biggest disaster for two years. Kitchener's elastic morale, frayed by alternating months of hope and disappointment, finally snapped. He shut himself up in his bedroom and refused to see anyone—or eat anything—for two days."[83]

But the Boer capacity and will to resist was dwindling, even among the hardliners. The small-scale successes, of which there were still many, were not moving things forward for the Boers. As Thomas Pakenham explains, "...it turned out that the Boers, as usual, were unable to turn a tactical victory to any strategic account."[84]

Kitchener's sweeps, coupled with the extensive introduction of concentration camps, blockhouses, and barbed wire, were limiting the Boers' scope for operations. The resistance now only comprised the hardliners, the "Bitter Enders," such as Christiaan de Wet and Koos de la Rey. The cost of continued resistance was too much for many Boers, and other commanders and fighters drifted back to their homesteads and farms. Some even joined the British.

The Boer political leadership put out more tentative feelers to the British to see what terms might be available. On April 11th, a train containing Botha, Smuts, de Wet, and Steyn arrived at the Pretoria station so the Boers and the British could begin discussions. On the same day, at the Battle of Rooiwal, the Boers suffered a serious defeat. The Boers were caught by superior British forces. In a bizarre twist of fate, this resulted in a massed cavalry charge by one and a half thousand Boers, who, by accident, had come across three thousand British who had previously been concealed by a ridge. It was a death or glory charge, with the Boers desperately gambling everything in the hope that the British might break and run. However, they did not, and it was the Boers who dispersed in retreat, leaving many bodies behind them, including General Potgieter.

---

serious. Apparently, the two generals became good friends as a result of this.
https://www.ladysmithhistoricalsociety.ca/histories/street-names/major-general-lord-methuen/

[83] Pakenham, T., *The Boer War*, (Abacus: London 2022), p.549.

[84] Pakenham, T., *The Boer War*, (Abacus: London 2022), p.550.

In mid-May, peace negotiations resumed. Before the Boers sat down with the British, they held their own private discussions to see what condition they were in (whether they could continue the fight) and how they should approach the talks. It was clear that the ability to offer further resistance was very low; the major problems were the lack of food, the lack of horses, and the poor conditions the Boer civilian population faced. This was also Kitchener's assessment of the Boer situation.[85]

The Boers, despite the emotional ties to the cause of independence and the two and a half years of suffering, had very little to bargain with. There appeared little hope of a large-scale, pro-Boer uprising in the Cape Colony (one of Milner's chief fears), and significant international support was not forthcoming. Some Boers joined the British forces. Zulu and other African tribes threatened the Boer population.[86]

On May 31st, 1902, at Vereeniging, the Boer delegation, by a voting margin of fifty-four in favor and six against, signed the peace agreement in front of Kitchener and the British representatives. The Boers accepted British sovereignty rather than independence, but they did ensure some elements of self-governance and administration. The British added a £3 million fund to begin immediate reconstruction in the two former Boer provinces. Within days, only 20,000 British soldiers remained of the 250,000 force that had chased the Boers all over South Africa.

The war was over.

---

[85] Pakenham, T., *The Boer War*, (Abacus: London 2022), p.566.
[86] Pakenham, T., *The Boer War*, (Abacus: London 2022), p.568.

Conclusion

The Second Boer War took place during a very turbulent time in international relations. Military technology and tactics were going through a massive upheaval. As a result, the war offered scenes that would not have been out of place in the Napoleonic Wars (shoulder-to-shoulder attacks) or modern conflicts from the 20th and even 21st centuries (trenches and machine guns).[87]

    The Boers were a curious opponent for the British. They were an enemy that the British always struggled to understand. The Boers were neither a conventional modern European army nor an African tribal force. As a result, the British, due to their rigid rules and tactics and a history of fighting disorganized tribal opponents, made some rather appalling mistakes. Nearly half a million British and colonial soldiers fought in the Boer War against a maximum of eighty to ninety thousand Boers. The sheer weight of British Empire resources was able to help to some degree. It was not until much later in the war that British commanders (and certainly not all of them) began to adapt, taking greater advantage of cover, concealment, mobility, smaller numbers, firepower, and movement. British counter-insurgency tactics were harsh but increasingly effective, with the introduction of blockhouses, barbed wire, and mobile columns that helped to isolate the Boers.

---

[87] There are photographs of Maxim machine guns currently being used by both sides in the Russo-Ukraine War.

Many military historians suggest that, without this painful lesson on the veld, the British Army would have performed much worse in France in 1914 against the German Army.

The Boer War also gave a darker indication of what "total war" would look like in the 20th century, particularly the widening scale of destruction. It showed how civilian populations would suffer worse than the armies. Concentration camps, refugees, starvation, and displacement were all tools to be used to undermine the enemy's will.

Casualty figures are hard to pin down with any degree of confidence. The Encyclopedia Britannica suggests 100,000 people died in total, including 20,000 British soldiers, 12,000 Boer fighters, and 26,000 Boer women and children. African deaths are not well recorded, but between ten thousand to twenty thousand might have died just in the concentration camps.[88] However, many other black Africans died in sieges, suffered starvation, or fought and died on both sides.

The former Boer provinces set about the business of reconstruction under British supervision, including getting the gold and diamond mines back up and running. A new Liberal government came to power in Britain in 1906 and took a more conciliatory approach to South Africa. The Transvaal and the newly named Orange River Colony received increasing measures of self-government in 1906 and 1907. Many former Boer commanders remained active in politics. For example, Louis Botha became the prime minister of the Transvaal. In 1910, the Union of South Africa was established from the Cape Colony, Natal, the Transvaal, and the Orange River. It was a self-governing British dominion that was to last until 1961.

The British/South African relationship remained mercurial. In late 1914, a Boer rebellion broke out. It was triggered by a handful of "Bitter Enders." Some even went as far as to call it the Third Boer War. It was short-lived and over in a matter of months. Prime Minister Louis Botha supported the British. He defeated the rebels without British military support (in late 1914, British forces were urgently needed in France) and invaded German South West Africa.

When the Second World War broke out, the Union of South Africa was in a dilemma. Some politicians wanted to be neutral. However,

---

[88] https://www.britannica.com/event/South-African-War/Peace

under Prime Minister Jan Smuts, the former Boer guerrilla commander, thousands of South African soldiers fought bravely alongside the forces of the British Empire in East Africa, North Africa, and Italy. Many others also served in the Royal Air Force.

On June 12th, 1944, Prime Minister Winston Churchill, the former military officer and journalist during the Boer War, sailed to Normandy to get a report from General Bernard Montgomery about the progress after the D-Day landings. Churchill was accompanied by Jan Smuts, who wore the uniform of a British field marshal. They must have had a lot to talk about.

Chronology[89]

7 October 1899 - British Army ordered to mobilize

9 October 1899 - Sir Redvers Buller appointed commander in chief in South Africa

11 October 1899 - Boer ultimatum expires

12 October 1899 - South African Republic invades Natal

13 October 1899 - Siege of Mafeking begins

15 October 1899 - Siege of Kimberley begins

21 October 1899 - Battle of Elandslaagte

2 November 1899 - Siege of Ladysmith begins

28 November 1899 - Battle of Modder River

10 December 1899 - Battle of Stromberg

11 December 1899 - Battle of Magersfontein

15 December 1899 - Battle of Colenso

18 December 1899 - Lord Roberts appointed commander in chief in South Africa

24 January 1900 - Battle of Spion Kop

15 February 1900 - Relief of Kimberley

18 February 1900 - Battle of Paardeberg

---

[89] Adapted from the chronology provided by the British National Army Museum, https://www.nam.ac.uk/explore/boer-war

27 February 1900 - Surrender of General Piet Cronje at Paardeberg

28 February 1900 - Relief of Ladysmith

13 March 1900 - British occupation of Bloemfontein

17 May 1900 - Relief of Mafeking

24 May 1900 - Annexation of the Orange Free State

29 May 1900 - Battle of Doornkop

31 May 1900 - British occupation of Pretoria

11-12 June 1900 - Battle of Diamond Hill

30 July 1900 - Surrender of General Marthinus Prinsloo in the Brandwater Basin

1 September 1900 - Annexation of the South African Republic

13 September 1900 - Lord Roberts calls on the Boers to surrender

29 September 1900 - Lord Kitchener succeeds Roberts as commander in chief

November 1900 - Concentration camps introduced

28 February 1901 - Kitchener and Louis Botha meet at Middelburg to discuss peace

15 September 1901 – Decision to send captured Boer leaders out of the country

21 September 1901 - Property of Boers still fighting to be sold

25 January 1902 - Dutch government offers to mediate

7 March 1902 - Battle of Tweebosch

12 April 1902 - Boer peace delegates meet Kitchener at Pretoria

31 May 1902 - Treaty of Vereeniging signed

Terminology

Battalion - British term for an organized battlefield grouping of fighting troops. The total official strength for a battalion in 1899 would have been around nine hundred soldiers, of which thirty or so would be officers. British infantry battalions were comprised of sub-units known as companies. There could be as many as eight companies, identified from A Company through to H Company, of around one hundred soldiers each in a full-strength battalion.

Battery - A combat grouping of artillery, usually comprising eight guns.

Boer - Farmer (originally from the Dutch word for farmer).

Brigade - A military grouping of forces for battlefield operations. A brigade is the smallest formation that is designed to be able to operate independently (i.e., it brings along all the supporting components that it will need, including supplies, engineers, bridging equipment, signals troops, headquarters, and intelligence troops). The concept was used extensively by the British during the Boer War. It is commonly comprised of four battalions, as well as all necessary supporting units. It is commanded by a brigadier, known in full as a brigadier general.[90]

Burgher - A Boer citizen, often used interchangeably to mean a Boer soldier.

---

[90] In modern terminology, this would also be known as a one-star general.

Corps – A British military formation, usually comprising between two to five divisions, depending on the theater and the mission. It would usually be commanded by a lieutenant general.[91]

Division – A larger British military formation, usually comprised of two or three brigades. This would be commanded by a Major General.[92]

Donga – A dry riverbed or gully with steep sides. It can serve as a trench-like defensive position and also allow hidden movements.

Drift – A ford or shallow crossing point of a river.

Flying column – British mobile force, mainly cavalry or mounted infantry, intended for fast movement.

Kommando or commando – Boer mounted military unit.

Kop or koppie – A hilltop or mountaintop.

Kraal – A defensive stockade of buildings.

Long Tom – Nickname for Boer Le Creusot 155mm heavy artillery.

Pom-pom – Maxim Nordenfelt heavy machine gun firing 37mm explosive shells.

Rand – Ridge of high ground.

Regiment – A military and/or administrative grouping of soldiers. The parent organization of British battalions providing support, logistics, and training. Each regiment had its own home location and base depot, either in Britain or in the local colony in which it was raised.

Shrapnel – An artillery shell designed by a British artillery officer, Lieutenant General Henry Shrapnel. The hollow shell was packed full of ball-shaped "bullets" to increase the lethality when the shell burst.

Veld – Flat grasslands.

---

[91] In modern terminology, this would also be known as a three-star general.
[92] In modern terminology, this would also be known as a two-star general.

Dramatis Personae

Robert Baden-Powell – British military commander at Mafeking during the siege. Founder of the British Boy Scout movement.

Louis Botha – Boer military commander and politician.

Redvers Buller – Commander of British forces in South Africa (replaced by Roberts in December 1899).

Joseph Chamberlain – Colonial Secretary.

Winston Churchill – Journalist, military officer, and later British prime minister during the Second World War.

Piet Cronje – Boer military commander.

John French – British major general, later commander in chief of the British Expeditionary Force in France during the First World War.

Mahatma Gandhi – Red Cross stretcher-bearer for the British Army, later a social activist and anti-colonial leader against British rule in India.

Leander Jameson – Responsible for the Jameson Raid from December 1895 to January 1896.

Piet Joubert – Former vice president to Paul Kruger, Boer military commander in the First and Second Boer Wars.

Herbert Kitchener – Chief of staff of the British Army in South Africa, later commander in chief (replaced Roberts in 1902).

Paul Kruger – President of the South African Republic (the Transvaal).

Alfred Milner – Cape Colony governor.

Koos de la Rey – Boer military commander.

Frederick Roberts – Commander of British forces in South Africa (replaced Buller in December 1899).

Cecil John Rhodes – Prime minister of the Cape Colony, mining magnate.

Jan Smuts – Boer military commander, prime minister in the later Union of South Africa, British Army field marshal during World War Two.

Martinus Steyn – President of the Orange Free State.

Christian de Wet – Commander in chief of the armed forces of the Orange Free State.

George Stuart White – Commander of the British forces in Natal and later of the British forces during the siege of Ladysmith.

If you enjoyed this book, a review on Amazon would be greatly appreciated because it would mean a lot to hear from you.

To leave a review:
1. Open your camera app.
2. Point your mobile device at the QR code.
3. The review page will appear in your web browser.

Thanks for your support!

Here's another book by Captivating History that you might like

SCRAMBLE FOR AFRICA

A CAPTIVATING GUIDE TO IMPERIAL RIVALRIES, HEROIC BATTLES, AND THE UNFOLDING LEGACY OF THE CONTINENT, INCLUDING THE ZULU WAR

CAPTIVATING HISTORY

Free Bonus from Captivating History (Available for a Limited time)

Hi History Lovers!

Now you have a chance to join our exclusive history list so you can get your first history ebook for free as well as discounts and a potential to get more history books for free!

Simply visit the link below to join.

Or, Scan the QR code!

captivatinghistory.com/ebook

Also, make sure to follow us on Facebook, X, and YouTube by searching for Captivating History.

Made in the USA
Columbia, SC
25 August 2024